HALLELUJAH!
THE WELCOME TABLE
A Lifetime of Memories with Recipes

Also by Maya Angelou

AUTOBIOGRAPHY

I Know Why the Caged Bird Sings

Gather Together in My Name

Singin' and Swingin' and Gettin' Merry Like Christmas

The Heart of a Woman

All God's Children Need Traveling Shoes

A Song Flung Up to Heaven

ESSAYS

Wouldn't Take Nothing for My Journey Now

Even the Stars Look Lonesome

POETRY

Just Give Me a Cool Drink of Water 'fore I Diiie

Oh Pray My Wings Are Gonna Fit Me Well

And Still I Rise

Shaker, Why Don't You Sing?

I Shall Not Be Moved

On the Pulse of Morning

Phenomenal Woman

The Complete Collected Poems of Maya Angelou

A Brave and Startling Truth

CHILDREN'S BOOKS

My Painted House, My Friendly Chicken, and Me

Kofi and His Magic

PICTURE BOOKS

Now Sheba Sings the Song

Life Doesn't Frighten Me

HALLELUJAH!
THE WELCOME TABLE
A Lifetime of Memories with Recipes

MAYA ANGELOU

Virago

VIRAGO

First published in Great Britain in October 2005 by Virago Press
First published in the United States in 2004 by Random House, Inc.

Copyright © Maya Angelou 2004
Photographs copyright © Sockeye Studios 2004

The moral right of the author has been asserted.

A CIP catalogue record for this book
is available from the British Library

ISBN 1 84408 163 X

Designed in 11pt Stempfel Garamond by
Geoff Green Book Design

Printed and bound in Italy

Virago Press
An imprint of
Time Warner Book Group UK
Brettenham House
Lancaster Place
London WC2E 7EN

www.virago.co.uk

DEDICATION

I dedicate this book to every wannabe cook who will
dare criticism by getting into the kitchen and stirring
up some groceries.

To O, who said she wanted a big pretty cookbook.
Well, honey, here you are.

ACKNOWLEDGEMENTS

To all the great cooks whose food I have eaten and whose recipes I have read and whose stories I have heard. My thanks to Bettie Burditte, Patricia Casey, Frances Berry, Sterling Baker, and Rosa Johnson Butler, who helped me at all hours for months to compile the recipes. I am proud that frustration did not cause them to move abroad and change their names. I thank my entire family for trusting me in the kitchen. And a salute to Brian Lanker, who helped me see clearly the images of foods that were becoming fuzzy in my memory.

Here's to Brian Daigle, who drove my bus so steadily across the U.S.A. that Lydia Stuckey and I could cook everything from baked acorn squash to zucchini gratinée.

Thank you all.

Maya Angelou

MEASUREMENTS

Please note that metric, imperial and cup measurements are given for the recipes. Follow one set of measures, not a mixture, as they are not interchangeable.

All spoon measures are level unless otherwise stated. Sets of measuring spoons are available in metric and imperial for accurate measurements.

Medium eggs should be used in the recipes, except where otherwise specified.

We have included cooking temperatures for electric and gas ovens. Remember if you have a fan-assisted oven that you need to reduce the oven temperature slightly (usually by around 20 degrees) and/or adjust the cooking times. Please refer to manufacturer's guidelines for more specific information on adjusting the temperature and time for your cooker, if applicable.

Some of the recipes in this book may contain raw or lightly cooked eggs – these recipes are not recommended for babies and young children, pregnant mums, the elderly and those convalescing.

CONTENTS

PIE FISHING   1
Lemon Meringue Pie ~ 7
Meringue ~ 7
Chicken and Dumplings ~ 8
Bouquet Garni ~ 9
Drop Dumplings ~ 9
Fried Yellow Summer Squash ~ 9
Green Peas and Lettuce ~ 10

THE ASSURANCE OF CARAMEL
CAKE   11
Caramel Cake ~ 19
Caramel Syrup ~ 20
Caramel Icing ~ 20
Coconut Cake ~ 21
Coconut Icing ~ 22
Chocolate Fudge ~ 22

MOMMA'S GRANDBABIES LOVE
CRACKLIN' CRACKLIN'   23
Crackling Corn Bread ~ 27
Momma's Rich Beef Stew ~ 28
Collard Greens ~ 29

POTATO SALAD TOWERS
OVER DIFFICULTIES   31
Cold Potato Salad ~ 36
Fried Chicken ~ 37
Snow-White Turnips ~ 38
Mustard and Turnip Greens with
    Smoked Turkey Wings ~ 38

Pickled Peaches ~ 39
Buttermilk Biscuits ~ 40

LIVER TO GROW ON   41
Liver and Onions ~ 46

RECIPES FROM ANOTHER COUNTRY   47
Wilted Lettuce ~ 51

INDEPENDENCE FOREVER   53
Fried Meat Pies ~ 58

EARLY LESSONS FROM A
KITCHEN STOOL   59
Bread Pudding ~ 64

MY BIG BROTHER'S SAVINGS
ACCOUNT   65
Bailey's Smothered Pork Chops ~ 69
Smoked Pork Chops ~ 70
Braised Cabbage with Ginger ~ 71
Cabbage with Celery and Water
    Chestnuts ~ 72

SHORT RIBS Á LA THE BIG EASY   73
Braised Short Ribs of Beef ~ 79

MOTHER'S LONG VIEW   81
Red Rice ~ 86
Roasted Capon ~ 86

GOOD BANANA, BAD TIMING   87
Banana Pudding ~ 92

READY-TO-WEAR TRIPE　　　93
Tripe à la Mode de Caen ~ 99
Red Tripe with White Rice ~ 100
Menudos (Tripe Stew) ~ 101

M.J. AND THE DOCTOR AND
MEXICAN FOOD　　　103
Tamales de Maiz con Pollo (Green
　Cornhusk Tamales with Chicken
　Filling) ~ 108

SAVING FACE AND SMOKING IN
ITALY　　　109
Roasted Turkey ~ 116
Corn Bread Stuffing ~ 117

HAUTE CUISINE À LA TABASCO 119
Veal Medallions ~ 124
Pâté ~ 125
Moulded Eggs Polignac ~ 126

ENGLISH, PLEASE　　　127
Onion Tart ~ 132

SWEET SOUTHERN MEMORIES 133
Spoon Bread ~ 138
Fried Apples ~ 138
Homemade Biscuits ~ 139
Sausage ~ 140

FOWL COMMUNICATION　　　141
Decca's Chicken, Drunkard
　Style ~ 145
Bob's Boston Baked Beans ~ 146

M. F. K. FISHER AND A WHITE BEAN
FEAST　　　147
Cassoulet ~ 152

FROM PIZZA TO CLAIBORNE AND
BACK　　　153
Beef Wellington ~ 160
Puffed Pastry ~ 161

Gazpacho ~ 161
Petit Pois ~ 162
Twice-Baked Potatoes ~ 163
Haricots Verts ~ 164
Vinaigrette ~ 164

SISTERLY TRANSLATION　　　165
Pickled Pig's Feet, or Souse ~ 169
Hog Head Cheese ~ 170

DOLLY AND SHERRY AND
MAKING SISTERS　　　171
Chicken Livers ~ 175
Buttered Noodles ~ 176

WRITER'S BLOCK　　　177
Éclairs ~ 182
Custard Filling ~ 183
Golden Whipped Cream ~ 183
Chocolate Syrup ~ 183

MASSACHUSETTS, TENNESSEE, AND
AN ITALIAN SOUP　　　185
Minestrone Soup ~ 190
Minnesota Wild Rice ~ 191

BLACK IRON POT ROAST　　　193
Black Iron Pot Roast ~ 198

OPRAH'S SUFFOCATED CHICKEN 199
Smothered Chicken ~ 204

ASHFORD SALAD '96　　　205
Tomato Soufflé ~ 209
Chakchouka (Moroccan Stew) ~ 210
Ashford Salad '96 ~ 211
Mixed Salad with Feta and Golden
　Raisins ~ 211

INDEX　　　212

PIE FISHING

My grandmother, who my brother, Bailey, and I called Momma, baked lemon meringue pie that was unimaginably good. My brother and I waited for the pie. We yearned for it, longed for it. Bailey even hinted and dropped slightly veiled suggestions about it, but none of his intimations hastened its arrival. Nor could anything he said stave off the story that came part and parcel with the pie.

Bailey would complain, "Momma, you told us that story a hundred times" or "We know what happened to the old woman" and "Momma, can we just have the pie?" (Momma always ignored his attempts to prevent her from telling the tale.) But if we wanted Momma's lemon meringue pie, we had to listen to the story:

There was an old woman who had made it very clear that she loved young men. Everyone in town knew where her interests lay so she couldn't get any local young men to come to her house. Old men had to be called to clean out her chimney or fix her roof or mend her fences. She learned to count on finding young strangers who were traveling through the area.

One Sunday morning there was a new young man in church sitting alone. Mrs. Townsend saw him and as soon as the last hymn was sung, before anyone else could reach him, she rushed over to his bench.

"Morning, I'm Hattie Townsend. What's your name?"

"George Wilson, ma'am."

She frowned a little.

"Anybody get to you?"

"No, ma'am. I don't know anyone here. Just passed by, saw the church, and stopped in." He had used the word ma'am out of courtesy.

She was all smiles again. "Well, then I'm inviting you, and I am a good cook, to my house for Sunday dinner. I have my own chickens and two cows, so my chickens are fresh and my butter is rich. I live in walking distance. Here is my address; come around this afternoon around three o'clock."

She patted him on the shoulder and left the church.

A few young men from the congregation rushed over.

"Mrs. Townsend invited you for dinner?"

"Yes."

"Well, I'm Bobby. Here's Taylor and this one is Raymond. We've all been to her house and she's a good cook."

The men started laughing.

"No, she's a great cook. It's just that after you eat, she pounces."

"Man, the lady can pounce."

The stranger said, "I don't mind a little pouncing."

They all laughed again. "But man, she's old. She's older than my mother."

"She's older than my grandmother."

"She's older than baseball."

The stranger said, "I'll eat dinner and after that I can take care of myself. Thanks, fellas, for warning me."

Bobby shouted, "Her lemon pie will make a rabbit hug a hound."

Taylor added, "Make a preacher lay his Bible down."

Meanwhile, Mrs. Townsend entered her house and went directly to her sewing box. She put on her glasses and took out a needle.

She walked back down the path to her house and stuck the needle in a tree.

She returned to the house and began to cook a chicken she had resting in the refrigerator. For the next hour she stirred pots and shifted pans, then she set her dining table for two. She had time to freshen up and change before her company came.

"Well, welcome, Mr. Wilson."

He was a little cooler than he had been at church.

She knew why but she also knew he hadn't eaten her cooking.

"The bathroom is here if you would like to freshen up. Dinner is not quite ready yet."

Of course everything was ready, but she wanted him to have time to breathe in the fine aromas floating in the air.

She served him chicken and dumplings. Chicken tender as mercy and dumplings light as summer clouds.

The side dishes were fried yellow summer squash and English peas.

He didn't care that he was eating as if he hadn't eaten in a month. She kept pressing him, "Eat some more, but save a place for dessert. Some people swear by my lemon meringue pie."

Between bites she thought she heard him mumble, "That's my favorite."

When he put his first bite of Mrs. Townsend's pie in his mouth, he was hers. He was ready to marry her or let her adopt him.

She sat opposite and watched as with each forkful he surrendered more.

After the second slice he would have followed her to the Sahara Desert.

She said, "Let's go out on the porch for the air."

He replied meekly, "Yes, ma'am."

Once they settled into the swing on the porch she said, "My goodness, night has fallen. It's quite dark."

"Yes, ma'am. It's dusk all right."

They swung a few times.

She asked, "What on earth is that shining down there in that tree?"

He squinted. "I can't hardly see a tree."

She said, "Yes, I see it. It's either a needle or a pin shining. Well, I do say. It's a needle."

He asked, "You can tell?"

She said, "Yes, I see the hole. I'll go get it."

He said, "Well, that proves you are not as old as they say you are. When you come back I may have some talk for you."

She stepped off the porch and went down the lane and retrieved the needle. When she came back she could hardly see the house, but she kept walking with her head up, triumph in her grasp.

She tripped in the darkness. After much fumbling she was able to stand erect. She saw that she had fallen over a cow that had lain down in the lane.

Mr. Wilson saw her fall, and he could see the cow. When she gave a little scream, he bounded off the porch to help her. Once she collected herself, he said, "Well, thank you for dinner. I have to go."

She asked, "Can't you stay for one more slice of pie?" The strength of the pie can be seen in the fact that he did stop to think about it.

She took his arm as if she wasn't going to give it back. He thought of the pie again and then the cow and the possible pouncing. He said, "No, ma'am," and snatched his arm and went away running. He escaped, but he never forgot the pie.

Each time, my grandmother laughed until tears flooded her cheeks. I think she knew Mrs. Townsend or someone very much like her.

Here is the recipe. In fact, here are the recipes for Mrs. Townsend's entire Young-Man-Catching Sunday Afternoon Dinner.

Best wishes.

LEMON MERINGUE PIE

Serves 6

200g/7oz/1 cup caster sugar

3 tablespoons cornflour (cornstarch)

⅛ teaspoon salt

350ml/12fl oz/1½ cups hot water

75g/3oz/1½ cups crumbs from soft-
   type bread (no crusts)

4 large egg yolks (reserve whites
   for Meringue)

15g/½oz/1 tablespoon butter

Grated rind of 1 medium lemon

Juice of 2 medium lemons

One 23cm/9in ready-baked shortcrust
   pastry case

Meringue (recipe follows)

Preheat oven to 200°C/400°F/Gas Mark 6.

In top part of double boiler, mix together well sugar, cornflour and salt. Stir in hot water and combine until smooth. Add breadcrumbs and cook over boiling water, stirring until smooth and thickened.

In small mixing bowl, beat egg yolks, and stir in a small amount of mixture. Then combine the two mixtures in double boiler, and cook over low to medium heat for 2 to 3 minutes. Add butter, lemon rind and lemon juice. Cool slightly.

Pour mixture into baked pastry case. Pile Meringue lightly on top, covering filling completely.

Bake for 10 minutes, or until lightly browned.

MERINGUE

4 large egg whites

⅛ teaspoon salt

1 teaspoon cream of tartar

4 tablespoons caster sugar

Whisk egg whites with salt until frothy. Gradually add cream of tartar and sugar. Whisk until stiff but not dry.

CHICKEN AND DUMPLINGS ∞

Serves 6 to 8

1 whole chicken (about 1.8kg/4lb), cut
    into pieces

6 chicken wings

1 large Spanish onion, chopped and
    sautéed but not browned

2 sticks celery, chopped

1 carrot, peeled and chopped

1 green (bell) pepper, seeded and
    chopped

Bouquet Garni (recipe follows)

Salt and freshly ground black pepper,
    to taste

Drop Dumplings (recipe follows)

Wash and pat dry chicken. Take flange off chicken wings.

Place chicken pieces and wings into large, heavy-based saucepan, and add water to cover 2.5cm/1 in above chicken. Add onion, celery, carrot, green pepper and Bouquet Garni. Season with salt and pepper. Allow mixture to simmer slowly for 1½ hours. Let cool. Remove any foam that has gathered on top of the broth.

Bring broth to a slight boil, and drop heaped tablespoons of dumpling batter into saucepan. Fill top of saucepan with dumplings. Cover pan, and simmer for 15 minutes – dumplings will rise. Baste dumplings, and continue simmering for another 5 minutes. Remove lid and baste dumplings. Serve hot on platter.

BOUQUET GARNI

3 bay leaves

8 black peppercorns

Tops from 2 sticks celery

1 teaspoon margarine

Cut double thickness of cheesecloth 15cm/6in wide. Place bay leaves, peppercorns, celery tops and margarine in center of cheesecloth. Pull corners of cheesecloth together, and tie with kitchen string.

DROP DUMPLINGS

225g/8oz/2 cups sifted plain
(all-purpose) flour

¼ teaspoon salt

2 heaped teaspoons baking powder

25g/1oz/2 tablespoons (¼ stick) butter

250ml/8fl oz/1 cup milk, plus
2 tablespoons milk

Sift flour, salt and baking powder into mixing bowl. Add butter, mixing with fingertips, then milk, until mixture is consistency of grainy cornmeal.

FRIED YELLOW SUMMER SQUASH

Serves 4

5 yellow squash or yellow courgettes
(zucchini)

1 tablespoon vegetable oil

15g/½oz/1 tablespoon butter

2 medium onions, diced and sautéed

Salt and freshly ground black pepper,
to taste

1 teaspoon fresh rosemary leaves,
finely chopped

Slice squash. In large skillet, sauté squash in oil and butter. When slightly brown, add onions. Season with salt and pepper. Cook over medium heat 3 more minutes, but do not allow squash to become mushy. Sprinkle with rosemary, and keep warm until served.

GREEN PEAS AND LETTUCE

Serves 4

1 small head iceberg lettuce

225g/8oz/2 cups fresh green peas
(shelled weight)

475ml/16fl oz/2 cups chicken or
vegetable stock

Salt and freshly ground black pepper,
to taste

300ml/½ pint/1¼ cups double (heavy)
cream, warmed

Remove heart from lettuce, and fill with peas. Tie up lettuce head with kitchen string to secure. Place in heavy-based saucepan with stock nearly to top of lettuce. Cover and steam until peas are tender, about 30 minutes. (Open the lettuce carefully, take one pea out, and test it.)

Remove string and discard. Open lettuce, season with salt and pepper, and pour cream over lettuce and peas. Serve at once.

THE ASSURANCE OF
CARAMEL CAKE

Quilting bees were eagerly anticipated by southern black women. They offered the only nonlabor, nonreligious occasions where women could gather and exchange all the communities' good and bad news. The women planned for weeks. Then they selected and cooked their favorite dessert dishes and brought them to the gathering. The bees were always held in the back of the store, which meant that Bailey and I could look forward to some delicious cakes and pies and, if the event took place in the summer, some luscious hand-cranked strawberry ice cream. Usually cranked by us.

Mrs. Sneed, the pastor's wife, would bring sweet potato pie, warm and a little too sweet for Momma's taste but perfect to Bailey and me. Mrs. Miller's coconut cake and Mrs. Kendrick's chocolate fudge were what Adam and Eve ate in the Garden just before the Fall. But the most divine dessert of all was Momma's Caramel Cake.

Momma would labor prayerfully over her selection, because she knew but would never admit that she and all the women were in hot competition over whose culinary masterpiece was the finest.

Momma could bake all the other women's dishes and often made them for the family, but not one of the other cooks would even dare the Caramel Cake (always to be spoken of in capital letters). Since she didn't have brown sugar, she had to make her own caramel syrup. Making her caramel cake took four to five hours, but the result was worthy of the labor. The salty sweetness of the caramel frosting along with the richness of the batter made the dessert soften and liquefy on the tongue and slip quietly down the throat almost without notice. Save that it left a memory of heaven itself in the mouth.

Of course Bailey and I were a little biased in Momma's favor, but who could have resisted the bighearted woman who was taller and bigger than most men yet who spoke in a voice a little above a whisper? Her hands were so large one could span my entire head, but they were so gentle that when she rubbed my legs and arms and face with blue-seal Vaseline every morning, I felt as if an angel had just approved of me.

I not only loved her, I liked her. So I followed her around. People began calling me her shadow.

"Hello, Sister Henderson, I see you got your shadow with you as usual." She would smile and answer, "I guess you got that right. If I go, she goes. If I stop, she stops. Yes, sir, I have me two shadows. Well, three by rights. My own and my two grandbabies."

I only saw Momma's anger become physical once. The incident alarmed me, but at the same time it assured me that I had great protection. Because of a horrible sexual violence I experienced when I was seven, I stopped talking to everyone but Bailey.

All teachers who came to Stamps to work at Lafayette County Training School had to find room and board with black families, for there were no boardinghouses where they could gain admittance.

All renting families acted as individual chambers of commerce for the newcomers. Each teacher was told of the churches and the preachers, of the hairdressers and barbers, of the white store downtown and the Wm. Johnson General Merchandise Store where they were likely to get accounts to tide them over between paychecks. The new teachers were also alerted to Mrs. Henderson's mute granddaughter and her grandson who stuttered seriously.

Summer was over and we returned to school with all the other children. I looked forward to meeting the new teacher of the fourth-, fifth-, and sixth-grade classes. I was really happy because for the first time Bailey and I were in the same classroom.

Miss Williams was small and perky. She reminded me of a young chicken pecking in the yard. Her voice was high-pitched. She separated the classes by row. Sixth-graders sat near the windows, fifth-graders were in the middle rows, and fourth-graders were near the door.

Miss Williams said she wanted each student to stand up and say his or her name and what grades they received at the end of the last semester.

She started with the sixth-graders. I looked at Bailey when he stood and said, "Bailey Johnson, Jr." At home he would make me fall out laughing when he said what he wished his whole name was: "Bailey James Jester Jonathan Johnson, Jr."

Because I didn't talk I had developed a pattern of behavior in classrooms. Whenever I was questioned, I wrote my answer on the blackboard. I had reached the blackboard in Miss Williams's room when the teacher approached me. We were nearly the same height.

She said, "Go back to your seat. Go on."

Bailey stood up over by the window.

He said, "She's going to write her name and grade on the blackboard."

Miss Williams said to me, "I've heard about you. You can talk, but you just won't talk."

The students, who usually teased me relentlessly, were on my side. They began explaining, "She never talks, Miss Williams, never." Bailey was nervous. He began to stutter. "My ... Maya can't talk."

Miss Williams said, "You will talk in my classroom. Yes, you will." I didn't know what to do. Bailey and the other children were trying to persuade her to allow me to write on the blackboard. I did not resist as she took the chalk out of my hand. "I know you can talk. And I will not stand for your silliness in my classroom." I watched her as she made herself angry. "You will not be treated differently just because your people own a store.

"Speak, speak." She was fairly shouting. Her hand came up unexpectedly and she slapped me. Truly, I had not known what to do when she was winding herself up to hit me, but I knew what I had to do the second her hand landed on my cheek. I ran. I ran out of the classroom with Bailey following shouting, "Wait, My, wait." I couldn't wait. I was running to Momma. He caught up with me on the porch of the store.

Momma, hearing the noise, opened the screen door.

"What happened? Why aren't you in school? Sister, why are you crying?"

Bailey tried to answer her, but his brain moved faster than his tongue could form the words.

I took my notebook and pencil and wrote, "Miss Williams slapped me because I wouldn't talk."

"She slapped you? Slapped? Where?"

Bailey said, "Fa ... fa ... fa ... face."

Momma told Bailey to go back to school. She said she and I would be coming soon.

Momma's calm voice and unhurried manner helped Bailey to settle down enough to speak.

"You want me to tell Miss Williams that you are coming?"

Momma answered, "I want you to go back to school and get your lesson." He looked at me once, saw that I had stopped crying, so he nodded and jumped off the porch and headed back up the hill.

"Sister, go to the well and put some fresh water on your face." I went around behind the store to the well.

When I returned to the porch Momma had put on one of her huge freshly washed, starched, sun-dried, and ironed aprons. In her hand she had the board that was slipped into pockets closing off the front door. We had a similar plank for the store, which we used every night to let customers know we were closed. I don't remember there being a lock for the house or the store.

Momma dropped the board into the slots, and in a second she was striding up the hill to the school.

I hurried beside, hoping to read her intentions in her face.

She looked as she always looked, serene, quiet. If she planned something unusual it did not register in her face.

She walked into the school building and turned around to me.

"Sister, show me your classroom."

I guided her to Miss Williams's room. She opened the door and Miss Williams walked up to Momma.

She asked, "Yes? May I help you?"

My grandmother asked, "Are you Miss Williams?"

Miss Williams said, "I am."

Momma asked, "Are you somebody's grandbaby?"

Miss Williams answered, "I am someone's granddaughter."

Momma said, "Well, this child here is my grandbaby." Then she slapped her. Not full force but hard enough for the sound to go around the room and to elicit gasps from the students.

"Now, Sister, nobody has the right to hit nobody in the face. So I am wrong this time, but I'm teaching a lesson." She looked at me. "Now find yourself a seat and sit down and get your lesson."

Momma left the room and it was suddenly empty and very quiet.

Miss Williams left the room for a few minutes. Not a word was spoken.

Miss Williams reentered and said, "Students, turn to lesson one on page one."

I looked at Bailey and he gave me the smallest nod. I turned to page one, lesson one.

No one spoke of the incident on the way home, and when I returned to the store Momma and Uncle Willie were sitting on the porch.

Uncle Willie said, "Sister, there's something on the kitchen table. Bring it out here please."

I went into the kitchen and on the chopping table stood the most wondrous Caramel Cake looking like paradise, oozing sweetness.

Carefully I brought it back to the porch and it was nearly worth being slapped just to hear Bailey gasp.

Uncle Willie said, "This cake can't pay you for being slapped in the face. Momma made it just to tell you how much we love you and how precious you are."

CARAMEL CAKE ∽

Serves 8

115g/4oz/½ cup (1 stick) soft butter

250g/9oz/1¼ cups caster sugar

50ml/2fl oz/¼ cup Caramel Syrup
   (recipe follows)

225g/8oz/2 cups sifted plain (all-
   purpose) flour

2 teaspoons baking powder

½ teaspoon salt

250ml/8fl oz/1 cup milk

2 large eggs

Caramel Icing (Frosting) (recipe
   follows)

Preheat oven to 190°C/375°F/Gas Mark 5. Line two 20cm/8in sandwich cake tins with greased non-stick baking paper.

In large mixing bowl, beat butter and add 200g/7oz/1 cup sugar gradually until light and fluffy. Beat in syrup.

In medium mixing bowl, sift flour, baking powder and salt together. Add sifted ingredients to creamed mixture, alternating with milk.

In separate medium mixing bowl, whisk eggs about 3 minutes, until foamy. Add remaining sugar, and whisk until there is a fine spongy foam. Stir into cake batter until blended.

Divide batter between prepared cake tins. Bake for about 25 minutes. Remove tins from oven. Gently press center of cake with forefinger. Cake should spring back when finger is removed. If it doesn't, return to oven for 10 minutes. Cool in tins for 10 minutes. Turn out onto cooling rack, and remove paper. Let cakes cool to room temperature before icing.

To assemble: Center one cooled cake on cake plate. Cover top and sides with generous helping of icing. Place second cake evenly on iced layer. Repeat icing procedure. Make certain that sides are completely iced. Cool in refrigerator until ready to serve.

CARAMEL SYRUP ⌒

200g/7oz/1 cup granulated sugar

250ml/8fl oz/1 cup boiling water

Heat sugar in heavy skillet over low heat. Stir constantly until melted to a brown liquid. When it bubbles over entire surface, remove from heat. Slowly add boiling water, stirring constantly. Pour into container and cool.

CARAMEL ICING (FROSTING) ⌒

75g/3oz/6 tablespoons (¾ stick) butter

225g/8oz/2 cups icing (confectioners') sugar

4 tablespoons double (heavy) cream

1½ teaspoons vanilla extract

Pinch of salt

Brown butter in heavy-based saucepan over medium heat – be vigilant or it will burn. Allow butter to cool. In large mixing bowl, add icing sugar, cream, vanilla extract and salt to the butter, and beat until smooth. If frosting is too stiff, add 1 tablespoon of half cream or full cream milk to thin.

COCONUT CAKE ∽

Serves 8

150g/5oz/⅔ cup soft butter

300g/11oz/1½ cups caster sugar

275g/10oz/2½ cups sifted soft (cake)
    or plain flour

2½ teaspoons baking powder

75ml/2½fl oz/⅓ cup milk

4 large egg whites

⅛ teaspoon salt

½ teaspoon cream of tartar

4 large egg yolks

1 teaspoon vanilla extract

1 teaspoon coconut flavouring

Coconut Icing (Frosting) (recipe
follows)

75g/3oz/1 cup desiccated (shredded
    sweet) coconut

Preheat oven to 180°C/350°F/Gas Mark 4. Line two 23cm/9in sandwich cake tins with greased non-stick baking paper. In large mixing bowl, cream butter and sugar, beating until light and fluffy.

In medium mixing bowl, sift together flour and baking powder. Add to creamed mixture, alternating with milk.

In separate medium mixing bowl, whisk egg whites until foamy. Whisk again for 2 minutes. Fold in salt and cream of tartar. Set aside.

In another medium mixing bowl, beat egg yolks. Add yolks to cake batter, then fold in whites, vanilla extract and coconut flavouring.

Pour batter into prepared cake tins. Bake for 30 to 35 minutes, or until cake springs back when center is pressed gently with forefinger. Cool in tins for 10 minutes; then turn out onto cooling rack, and remove paper. Let cakes cool to room temperature.

To ice, place one cake on cake plate, and spread icing on top. Sprinkle some desiccated coconut on top of icing. Place second cake onto first cake, and cover entire cake with icing. Sprinkle coconut on top of cake, and place coconut on sides of cake also. Refrigerate, and serve cold.

COCONUT ICING (FROSTING) ⌒

600ml/1 pint/2½ cups whipping
   cream
50g/2oz/½ cup icing (confectioners')
   sugar
1 teaspoon coconut flavouring

In medium mixing bowl, whip cream until frothy. Add sugar and coconut flavouring, and whip until it holds stiff peaks.

CHOCOLATE FUDGE ⌒

Makes about 10 pieces

600g/1lb 5oz/3 cups granulated sugar
750ml/1¼ pints/3 cups milk
2 tablespoons golden syrup or liquid
   glucose or glucose syrup
175g/6oz plain chocolate, broken
   into squares
40g/1½ oz/3 tablespoons butter
1 teaspoon vanilla extract
115g/4oz/1 cup chopped pecans
   (optional)

Butter 20cm/8in square shallow cake tin.

In large, heavy-based saucepan, bring sugar, milk, golden syrup and chocolate to a boil.

Put a drop of mixture in 250ml/8fl oz/1 cup of ice-cold water. When the drop forms a soft ball, remove from heat. If ball does not form, continue cooking and repeat until ball forms.

Stir butter and vanilla extract into hot mixture. Cool. When saucepan with chocolate mixture has cooled to a lukewarm temperature, beat mixture with wooden spoon until it loses its gloss and becomes thick. If you want nuts, stir in pecans before mixture cools completely. Pour into tin and cool completely. Cut in desired size squares.

Fried Chicken

Lemon Meringue Pie

Caramel Cake

Crackling Corn Bread

Cold Potato Salad

Mustard and Turnip Greens with Smoked Turkey Wings

Smoked Pork Chops

Braised Short Ribs of Beef

MOMMA'S GRANDBABIES
LOVE CRACKLIN' CRACKLIN'

E ach year after the first frost, men and women wearing heavy clothes and carrying rifles and sawed-off shotguns stalked around inside the store buying peanut patties and candy bars.

Bailey called them the killing crew because they went around the neighborhood killing all the hogs and cows that had been selected for slaughter.

For the next two weeks, or as long as our icebox could keep the meat, we would be sure that Momma was going to cook some exquisite fresh beef and pork dishes.

She told me that she could cook a whole hog and make people love to eat it. "Everything but its hooves." She said when it came to hogs, poor people had to learn how to use everything "from the rooter [its snout] to the tooter [its tail]."

The neighborhood women would bring the hog heads and intestines to the store. They would put the heads on tables that had been set up outside between the wells and the iron pots where we washed out clothes. They would carry the intestines far beyond the outdoor toilet and empty them in a hole in the ground, dug for that purpose.

The stench was horrible, but Momma never allowed me to leave the spot and return to the store where there were the aromas of oranges and apples. "You have to know how to do this, Sister. All poor people need to know how to do some of everything, and a poor colored woman even more so. Don't turn your nose up at anything except evil."

While I bustled about helping in the stinking miasmic odor, I tried to think of the rich stew that Momma always served with crackling bread. But it was the thought of crackling bread itself that made me forget the smell of raw intestines.

Momma salted and roasted a large pan full of pork skin, which would become so crisp that it crackled. The fat rendered from the meat was stored to be used later for cooking and making soap.

She always gave a few crispy pieces of the skin to her grandbabies and to Uncle Willie, but most of the cracklings were saved for her great beef stew or until she cooked and served a large pot of collard greens. Then she'd bring out a giant pan of corn bread filled with cracklings.

The greens and stew dinner, which was always served with raw onions, pickled beets, and a jar of pepper sauce, was one of my favorite winter meals.

Although two adults and two children would share the food, Momma never reduced the size of the bread she gave us. I preferred Momma's crackling corn bread over other people's Sunday cake.

CRACKLING CORN BREAD ✆

Serves 8

225g/8oz/2 cups white cornmeal or
   maizemeal

25g/1oz/¼ cup sifted plain (all-
   purpose) flour

1 tablespoon caster sugar

½ teaspoon salt

4 teaspoons baking powder

350ml/12fl oz/1½ cups milk, plus 2
   tablespoons milk

2 large eggs, beaten well

25g/1oz/2 tablespoons (¼ stick) butter,
   melted

225g/8oz crisp cracklings,* broken
   into 1cm/½in pieces

Preheat oven to 180°C/350°F/Gas Mark 4.
Grease a 20 x 20 x 5cm/8 x 8 x 2in tin.

Mix dry ingredients in mixing bowl; stir in
milk and eggs. Pour in butter, and add
cracklings. Pour mixture into prepared tin
and bake for 1 hour, or until brown and
firm.

*   Cracklings are called chicharones in
    Spanish and can be found in Latino
    grocery stores.

MOMMA'S RICH BEEF STEW ⌒

Serves 8

1.3kg/3lb chuck or braising steak, cut
   into bite-size pieces

Salt and freshly ground black pepper,
   to taste

50g/2oz/½ cup plain (all-purpose) flour

75ml/2½fl oz/⅓ cup vegetable oil

750ml/1¼ pints/3 cups water

1 teaspoon salt

½ teaspoon freshly ground black
   pepper

3 bay leaves

1 teaspoon chopped fresh parsley

1 onion, cut into large pieces

2 turnips, peeled and cut into large
   pieces

1 swede (rutabaga), peeled and cut
   into large pieces

2 white potatoes, peeled and cut into
   large pieces

1 parsnip, peeled and cut into large
   pieces

3 carrots, peeled and cut into large
   pieces

1 green (bell) pepper, seeded and cut
   into large pieces

Season beef with salt and pepper, then dredge in flour. Pour oil into large saucepan over medium heat. Add beef, and brown on all sides in oil. Add water, salt and pepper, bay leaves and parsley, and cook simmering for 1 hour.

Add vegetables. Check seasoning, and bring vegetables and meat back to boil. Cover stew and cook on medium. When meat and vegetables are tender, take stew off heat and let rest for 15 to 20 minutes.

Serve with good Italian bread or Crackling Corn Bread (p. 27).

COLLARD GREENS (SPRING GREENS)

Serves 4

2 smoked turkey wings

3 bunches tender spring greens or
   kale (collards) (the greens are
   better if they are picked after the
   first frost)

1 sweet onion, chopped

2 fresh hot red chillies (peppers)

Salt and freshly ground black pepper,
   to taste

1 tablespoon granulated sugar

In large saucepan, boil turkey wings in water to cover for 1 hour.

Pick and wash greens, and discard large stems. Chop leaves coarsely.

Add all remaining ingredients to pan. Simmer for 1½ hours, adding water if needed. When greens are done, they can be served with Crackling Corn Bread (p. 27).

POTATO SALAD TOWERS
OVER DIFFICULTIES

We were members of the CME Church and for years I thought the initials stood for Colored Methodist Episcopal Church. Then I was told that the letters described the Christian Methodist Episcopal Church. Later I discovered I had been right the first time. But in Arkansas, and possibly in all the states, there were Presiding Elders, who were the crème de la crème, and they wouldn't have it otherwise.

The pompous Presiding Elder who served our region would arrive in town on horseback or, on the rare occasion, in a car, always with someone else driving. He would stay with other parishioners, but at every three-month visit he told Bailey and me that until our arrival he was always put up by Mother Henderson and Superintendent Johnson. (Uncle Willie was superintendent of the Sunday school.) We never knew what to say. Did he think we should get back on the train and return to parents who obviously had no place for us in their lives?

To say Bailey and I hated the Presiding Elder could not describe our bitter loathing for the puffed-up man who had no sensitivity to two wayfaring motherless and fatherless children.

He didn't sleep at Momma's house, but he took every meal there, and took is the correct word. Because of him, Bailey and I spent the most embarrassing hour of our lives, and to add insult to injury we became very sick.

Piss Ant, as Bailey called him, came round as usual after Sunday services. I brought him a face basin with water from the well so he could wash, but he hardly dipped his hand in the water, nor did he say thank you. I turned to go in the kitchen to help Momma, but I saw Bailey had seen Piss Ant's behavior.

Momma sent me to the garden to pick and wash lettuce. She had made her delicious potato salad. She chipped off a corner from a block of ice and pulverized it with a hammer. She put the lettuce in a pretty dish and laid crushed ice between the leaves.

When Momma called everyone in for Sunday dinner, the table was powerful with her delectables spread from end to end. There was the most golden-brown fried chicken, string beans with little potatoes, dark green turnip leaves with snow-white turnips, pickled peaches, and a platter of her buttermilk biscuits called cat heads because of their size. But the star of that show was the potato salad. Momma had mixed all the ingredients, then mounded the salad high above the top of the bowl. She had hard-boiled four double-yolk eggs and cut them in half and pushed them down into the potato mixture; then she placed crisp cucumber circles around the inside edges of the bowl.

Each person was supposed to pick up the fork in the lettuce bowl and take one leaf up, let it drip in the bowl, then place it on the salad plate just to the left of the dinner plate. Then a spoon of potato salad would be placed on the lettuce leaf. That was how we did it, how everybody did it except for the Presiding Elder. He glanced at the chicken and immediately took the three largest pieces. Then he used his own fork to serve himself potato salad.

Bailey cleared his throat and asked, "Would you like some lettuce?" Piss Ant was so used to ignoring children that he didn't even look at Bailey. He picked up the potato salad and fished out three of the halves of double-yolk eggs and put them on his plate beside the chicken. Then he completed filling his plate with the salad.

His mouth was so stuffed we could hardly understand him. "Save me some greens, sure have a soft spot for greens."

Bailey's face was a mask of angry disgust, and I knew he was going to do something. Just what, I wasn't sure. When Momma looked at her grandson, she also had a premonition.

Bailey hesitated only a second. Using the lettuce fork, he speared every leaf in the bowl, held it up to drip, and then put the whole thing on his plate.

Momma reared back and pursed her lips. She didn't speak. She turned and started to prepare Uncle Willie's plate. Bailey looked at me. I wanted to laugh but didn't dare, but I was pleased that he had the nerve to get that Presiding Elder good. I did give Bailey a little nod and he nodded back. Then he took the whole stack of lettuce and started to put it back into its receptacle. Momma said, "No, sir, little master, you will eat every bit of that lettuce before you get up from this table."

Momma didn't like the Presiding Elder either, but she was a stickler for the way to do things and the ways they shouldn't be done.

Bailey sat back in his chair and surveyed the situation. Then he pulled up to the table, and taking one forefinger he flicked one of the leaves into his lap, slid it over to me, and got one more himself. He showed me how to roll the leaf like a cigarette and munch it.

We ate the entire bowl of lettuce – and only the lettuce – for Sunday dinner. After the Presiding Elder left, Momma and Uncle Willie sat on the porch laughing. They would not admit to us that they had been laughing at Bailey, but Momma called us outside.

"Now, young missy and young master, I know your stomachs are upset. I've seen how many times you went out to the little outhouse. You didn't have to make yourselves sick. I have told you never be concerned at how much others may have. I always keep something in the kitchen for Grandma and the children."

That evening she gave us chicken from the oven and potato salad from the icebox.

COLD POTATO SALAD ∞

Serves 6 to 8

12 medium potatoes, peeled, diced
and cooked

1 medium onion, finely chopped

115g/4oz/1 cup finely diced celery

115g/4oz/1 cup chopped gherkins (dill
pickles)

225g/8oz/1 cup sweet relish, drained

8 large hard-boiled eggs, 4 chopped,
4 whole

Salt and freshly ground black pepper,
to taste

350ml/12fl oz/1½ cups mayonnaise

Chopped fresh parsley, to garnish

Combine potatoes, onion, celery, gherkins, relish and chopped eggs. Season with salt and pepper, and add mayonnaise. Chill for several hours. Just before serving, halve the remaining 4 eggs, and place on salad as garnish. Sprinkle salad with chopped parsley, and serve at once.

FRIED CHICKEN ∞

Serves 4

900g/2lb chicken

250ml/8fl oz/1 cup lemon juice

1 teaspoon salt

½ teaspoon freshly ground black
  pepper

115g/4oz/1 cup plain (all-purpose)
  flour

475ml/16fl oz/2 cups vegetable oil

Wash and pat dry chicken. Cut into pieces, place in a container, and add lemon juice. Put in refrigerator, covered, for 1 hour. Rinse, dry, and season with salt and pepper. Dredge chicken in flour.

In a large heavy-based saucepan, heat oil. Add chicken pieces, and cover. Fry on high heat until brown on both sides.

Reduce heat to low-medium, cover, and cook for 30 minutes.

Remove from heat, and drain on paper towels. Serve hot.

SNOW-WHITE TURNIPS ∞

Serves 4

8 small turnips, peeled

6 whole cloves

⅛ teaspoon salt

1 tablespoon granulated sugar

25g/1oz/2 tablespoons (¼ stick) butter

Place turnips, cloves and salt in a heavy saucepan. Cover with water. Boil until turnips are tender, about 20 to 30 minutes. Remove from stove, drain, and discard cloves. Add sugar, and stir until sugar dissolves. Add butter, and stir to melt. Serve at once.

MUSTARD AND TURNIP GREENS WITH SMOKED TURKEY WINGS ∞

Serves 6

2 smoked turkey wings

1.3kg/3lb mustard greens or spring greens

450g/1lb young, tender turnip greens

½ teaspoon granulated sugar

Salt, to taste

Place turkey wings in large saucepan, and cover with water. Boil until nearly tender, about 45 minutes to 1 hour.

Wash and drain greens. Put in pan with cooked meat. Add sugar and season with salt. Add enough water to cover, and simmer until tender.

Drain and reserve liquid, which is called 'pot liquor' and will be very good the next day with corn bread. Remove meat from bones, chop, and add to greens. Serve at once.

PICKLED PEACHES ∞

Serves 6

6 medium nearly ripe peaches,
   peeled and stoned

150g/5oz/¾ cup granulated sugar

⅛ teaspoon salt

120ml/4fl oz/½ cup cider vinegar

250ml/8fl oz/1 cup orange juice

1 tablespoon whole cloves

2 cinnamon sticks

Put peaches in large saucepan, add sugar, salt, vinegar, orange juice, cloves and cinnamon sticks, and cover with water. Boil for 30 minutes. Take off stove, and let cool. Put in refrigerator in its own liquid. Discard cloves and cinnamon. Serve cold.

BUTTERMILK BISCUITS ∽

Makes about 2 dozen biscuits

450g/1lb/4 cups plain
   (all-purpose)flour

½ teaspoon salt

6 teaspoons baking powder

1 teaspoon bicarbonate of soda
   (baking soda)

175g/6oz/1 cup lard

475ml/16fl oz/2 cups buttermilk

Plain (all-purpose) flour, for sprinkling

Preheat oven to 190°C/375°F/Gas Mark 5.

Sift flour with salt, baking powder and bicarbonate of soda. Cut in or rub in lard until mixture resembles coarse cornmeal. Add buttermilk, and stir until dough leaves side of bowl.

Turn dough out onto a lightly floured board, and knead until smooth. Roll out to 1cm/½in thickness, and cut into 5cm/2in rounds. If there is no biscuit cutter at hand, use a water glass. (Turn glass upside-down, dust rim in flour, and cut biscuits.)

Bake on un-greased baking sheet for 20 to 25 minutes, or until biscuits are golden brown. Transfer to wire rack to cool.

LIVER TO GROW ON

I n Stamps, women preserved everything that would submit to the process. After the first frost, when men killed the hogs and cows selected for slaughter, Momma, with the aid of the missionary ladies of the Christian Methodist Episcopal Church, would prepare the meat for sausage. I enjoyed watching them. They would grind the raw pork, then squeeze their arms elbow deep in the ground meat, mixing it with gray nose-opening sage, pepper and salt, and red pepper. They often fried tasty little samples for all obedient children who brought wood for the slick black stove. The men chopped off the larger pieces of pork and laid them in the smokehouse to begin the curing process. They opened the knuckle of the hams with their deadly-looking knives, took out a certain round, harmless-looking bone ("It could make the meat too bad"), and rubbed coarse brown salt that looked like fine gravel into the flesh, and watched as the blood popped to the surface.

Throughout the year, until the next frost, we took our meals from the smokehouse, the chicken coop, the shelves of canned goods, and the little garden that lay cousin-close to the store. There were choices on the shelves that could set a hungry child's mouth to watering. Green beans, snapped always the right length; collards; cabbage; juicy, sweet red tomato preserves that came into their own on steaming buttered biscuits; and sausage, beets, berries, and every fruit grown in Arkansas.

But at least twice yearly Momma would feel that her grandbabies needed fresh meat in their diets. We were then given money – pennies, nickels, and dimes entrusted to Bailey – and sent to the butcher to buy liver. The butcher shop was in the white part of town.

Crossing our area of Stamps, which in childhood's narrow measure seemed a whole world, obliged us by custom to stop and speak to every black person we met. Bailey also felt constrained to spend a few minutes playing with each friend. There I felt a special joy in going through the black area with time on our hands and money in our pockets. (Bailey's pockets were as good as my own.) But the pleasure fled when we reached the white part of town. Suddenly we were explorers walking without weapons into man-eating animals' territory.

We never turned to look at the houses we passed, nor did we really speak to each other once we were in enemy territory. We solemnly moved forward to our goal.

At the butcher shop we were lucky if no one came in. All whites were served before us, even if the butcher was half into our order. He would put our meat on the side and serve the white customer. In fact, a black maid or cook would be served before us, because her order was intended for white people. Bailey and I would stand around, never looking at each other, until there were no more calls on the butcher's time. Then we would get the liver Momma wanted to cook for our health and make our way back across the white zone I considered the frozen tundra, again wending through the black residential area where every house seemed to sing "Welcome" and on to the store and Momma and the hot skillet. The aromas of fried bacon and onions told us that all of them – the skillet, the stove, and Momma – had been waiting for the liver.

The liver dinner marked the only time when my grandmother and Uncle Willie let us have the best parts of the meat. They both chose small portions.

Momma said, "You are all growing. Liver is good for your

bones and your blood. So go on, eat it. You'll be better for it."

Twenty years had to pass before I could honestly say I loved liver well prepared. Bailey never came to accept it. But we chewed it and swallowed it, and it helped us to grow and maybe it did make us better human beings.

LIVER AND ONIONS ∽

Serves 6

450g/1lb back bacon rashers

5 medium onions, sliced

2 tablespoons plain (all-purpose) flour

1 teaspoon salt

½ teaspoon freshly ground black
  pepper

450g/1lb thinly sliced calves' liver

2 tablespoons vegetable oil

175ml/6fl oz/¾ cup water

Fry bacon in large skillet on medium heat, and remove from heat. Do not discard grease. Place bacon on paper towels to drain.

Using same skillet, cook onions in bacon fat until golden brown. Remove from heat, and place on paper towels to drain.

Mix together flour, salt and pepper, and dust liver with mixture. Heat oil in a large skillet, and fry liver lightly until browned on both sides. Remove liver and pour water into hot skillet. Scrape bottom of skillet. Season with salt and pepper if desired. Pour hot broth over liver. Serve at once with onions and crisp bacon.

RECIPES FROM ANOTHER COUNTRY

My grandmother did not subscribe to the Lafayette County *Democrat* newspaper, saying, "It is written by white folks, about white folks, for white folks."

We received *The Chicago Defender* and *The Pittsburgh Courier* newspapers although they were published in the far-away northern cities and arrived by mail at least a week late.

However, once a month, the *Democrat* published a women's page. The page held notices of weddings, engagements, and a few recipes that were sent in by readers with their names attached. Momma knew all the names and the maids who worked for them.

On the morning when the women's page was published, as the maids passed the store on their way to work, Momma would choose one.

"Sister Bishop, I hope you'll be able to bring me that page this evening."

The woman would smile, proud to have been chosen. "Yes, ma'am, Sister Henderson. Be glad to."

The other women in the group would compliment the chosen one amid much laughter. That evening the maid would bring a folded newspaper page, and Momma would take a Babe Ruth from the icebox or a peanut patty from the candy counter.

"You know I'm not trying to pay you. Just saying thank you."

Momma would sit down and gingerly put on her glasses. Immediately she would start tsking. (In the African American community, that gesture is called sucking your teeth.)

I would wait for her comments.

"Uh-huh-huh, these white folks. What will they stop at next?" She wagged her head. "They're making gravy with beer. You know what beer is, Sister?"

I would write, "Yes, ma'am. It's white lightning."

"That's right, uh-huh. You ready to start?"

We sat together under the lamplight so many nights copying recipes that I can pull a perfect image of me and Momma bending over the kitchen table, scrutinizing the news page.

Momma said, "Now, here is one for you. It's called wilted lettuce. Don't that beat all? I have to buy ice to make my lettuce crisp up, and here is a recipe for wilted lettuce.

"This cook didn't know all she had to do to make this dish is wash the lettuce and leave it on the counter. It will wilt for you in thirty minutes."

Then she thought again. "We have some nice lettuce in the garden. I'm going to make this dish tomorrow."

The next day we sat down to Momma's version of wilted lettuce, and much to her surprise we all enjoyed it. I ate the silken side dish and wondered about the white woman who lived in the white part of town about a mile from the black area, which was still called the Quarters.

Would she think that a black grandmother was feeding her grandchildren the same dish she was offering to her privileged family?

Would she resent the grandmother or just shrug her shoulders and say, "Let them help themselves"?

I'd like to think she shrugged.

WILTED LETTUCE ∽

Serves 4 to 6

6 rashers back bacon

6–8 spring (green) onions (white and
   green parts), sliced

1 tablespoon caster sugar

¼ teaspoon salt

75ml/2½fl oz/⅓ cup vinegar

250ml/8fl oz/1 cup water

¼ teaspoon freshly ground black
   pepper

2 heads round (Boston) or Little Gem
   (Bibb) lettuce, leaves washed and
   separated

Cut bacon into small pieces, and fry in medium skillet until crisp. Remove from heat, and drain on paper towels. Add spring onions, sugar, salt, vinegar, water and pepper to bacon fat in skillet. Cook over medium heat for 5 minutes.

Put lettuce into salad bowl. Pour onion mixture over lettuce, and stir. Top with crisp bacon, and serve immediately.

INDEPENDENCE FOREVER

In 1903, Momma had been married five years and had two sons. One bright morning, her husband told her that he was leaving. He explained that he had received a call – the Call – to preach. To study and prepare for that awesome responsibility, he had to travel to Ada, Oklahoma, where an elderly preacher he had met at a conference would school him. Years later Annie Henderson found that the old Oklahoma preacher had had a beautiful and marriageable daughter and that my grandfather quickly began to court her. When it was legally possible, he married the daughter and never returned to Arkansas.

My grandmother was left with a two-room shack, a lively four-year-old who would later become my father, and a two-year-old boy who was crippled.

For most of her life Annie Henderson blamed herself for Uncle Willie's condition. As a one-year-old he had crawled out of the house and had fallen off the porch to the ground.

No amount of doctors were able to convince my grandmother that Uncle Willie's paralysis was caused by a neurological malady rather than by what she thought of as her neglect.

She also laid my grandfather's departure to his displeasure at having a crippled son. So again, she was to blame.

She looked around at her situation. She was a colored woman in the South at the beginning of the twentieth century. She had herself and her sons to feed, house, and clothe. She would not work as a maid, for that would mean leaving her tots, especially her crippled one, in someone else's care. She decided to make use of the two largest employers in Stamps. They were the cotton gin, and three miles away, the lumber mill. She devised a plan that would let her make money and at the same time mostly stay at home with her "darlings."

At night she would cook and then grind and season ham and chicken and also make a batter for her cakes. Sunrise found her kneading the dough and placing the meat in the center of each pastry. Midmorning she walked from her house, leaving a young girl to watch her boys for three hours.

Carrying her fresh raw pies, her coal pot, lard, and a fold-up chair, she would arrive at the factory. She placed herself and supplies on the ground adjacent to the door the black workers used. She would begin frying pies a half hour before noon.

She told me many times that nothing sounds as loud as the dinner bell and nothing smells as good as fresh fried pies. She had a bell that she rang seconds after the noon siren sounded.

She sold the pies hot at the cotton gin for five cents. She would wrap any leftovers in a fresh tea towel, and leaving her cooking utensils under the care of a child hired for that purpose, she would run three miles to the lumber mill and offer the tepid pies for three cents. But believing in fair play and being a good businesswoman, the establishment that received lukewarm pies on one day would be her first stop the next noon. Her customers appreciated her cooking, her promptness, and her sense of fairness.

After a few years of serving the pies in both unbreathable summer heat and bone-shaking winter cold, Momma built a little hut equidistant between the two hives of commercial activity. Then at noontime the hungry workers would run to her to get their steaming chicken and cured ham pies.

Momma told me, "Sister, the world might try to put you on a road that you don't like. First stop and look behind you. If nothing back there makes you want to return, then look ahead. If nothing ahead beckons you enough to keep you going, then you have to step off that road and cut yourself a brand-new path."

The hut became a store in which I grew up. It remained in use for over sixty years.

FRIED MEAT PIES ∽

Serves 8

1 quantity Buttermilk Biscuits dough (p. 40)

275g/10oz/2 cups cooked finely chopped pork or chicken

Salt and freshly ground black pepper, to taste

Pinch of ground cinnamon

¼ teaspoon dried red pepper or chilli flakes

2–3 medium onions, caramelized (1 cup caramelized onions) (see below)

5 tablespoons vegetable oil

Roll out dough to 5mm/¼in thickness. Cut out circles, using salad plate or side plate. Season meat with salt and pepper, and add cinnamon and red pepper flakes. Place 2 tablespoons of meat off-center on dough circle. Put ½ teaspoon caramelized onions on meat. Fold dough to make a half-moon shape. Seal pie by pressing edges with fork tines. Refrigerate for 1 hour. Fry in 3 tablespoons oil on both sides on medium heat until golden brown.

To caramelize onions: Put 2 tablespoons of oil in frying pan, and add thinly sliced onions. Cook over medium-high heat, stirring constantly. When onions begin to brown, turn heat down. Continue to stir. Onions will become dark golden brown. Remove from heat.

EARLY LESSONS FROM A
KITCHEN STOOL

My mother, Vivian Baxter, was a great believer in self-reliance. Each tub should sit on its own bottom and each shoulder should be pressed to its own wheel.

My six-year-old son, Guy, and I were between addresses. That was how we described our condition when we lost one apartment and before we found another. In the meantime, of course, we went across town to my mother's house.

When I was seventeen and Guy was two months old, we lived with my mother in her fourteen-room house on Post Street in San Francisco. Then one morning I announced my plans to move. I told her that I had found a job and two rentals with cooking privileges and that the landlady would babysit my child. She controlled her surprise and said, "All right, but when you cross over my doorsill, remember you have been raised. Throughout life you will have to make many adjustments and even some compromises, but don't let anybody raise you. You know the difference between right and wrong. Do right. You've been raised.

"And remember this," she added. "You can always come home."

Whenever the world was too much with me late and soon, I returned to Vivian Baxter's house. I didn't savor not sitting on my own bottom and not putting my own shoulder to my own wheel, but I was never made uncomfortable returning to her.

She treated each return as a welcome opportunity to teach me something she had overlooked or that I had not understood. She relished one incident, which she said could only have taken place in her kitchen.

Guy sat at the kitchen table, watching her cook. He kept up a running chatter about school, his playmates, and his teachers, and he filled his conversation with his requests that his grandmother make a dessert for me.

He told her how hard I worked, how at this very moment I was probably seeing about an apartment, and how I deserved a dessert. A good dessert made for me by my mother.

Mother had had just about enough of that. "If she needs a dessert why don't you make it for her?"

"Oh, Grandma, I'm only six years old."

Mother said, "If you are old enough to try to bully me into making something for your mother, then you are old enough to make it yourself. Do you want to try?"

He laughed and said, "Sure."

She said she would show him how to make a bread pudding, after he washed his hands. "Cleanliness is next to godliness" was my mother's mantra. Mother set him on a kitchen stool so he could reach the sink.

"A good cook washes his hands ten times an hour; a great cook, twenty times."

Each time he touched a piece of food he climbed up onto the stool and washed his hands.

She let him butter stale bread, which was then placed in the oven to toast, and she showed him how to break eggs without dropping shells into the mixing bowl.

He whisked milk and then sugar into the eggs. He put raisins in warm water so they could plump.

There was an undeniable air of secret happenings when I entered the house that night. I looked at Mother, and her smile was like a promising but sealed envelope, and Guy was about to explode. I had to give them their due.

"What's going on? What have you people been doing?"
Mother said, "Ask your son."

"Well, Guy? What's the news?"

"Mom, well … I can't tell you until after dinner. Are you ready to eat right now? We can sit down and have dinner. Then we can have dessert. Oooo-weee." He spoke so fast he hardly had time to breathe.

He could not sit still at the dinner table.

Mother finally told him the dessert was cool enough and he could bring it out.

The baked bread pudding was puffed up and toasty brown, but I only had eyes for Guy. He strutted and preened. Pride and self-congratulations were his shoulder pads, and he nearly had to put both hands over his mouth to keep from blurting out his achievement.

When Mother placed the bread pudding in front of her to serve it, he could hold off no longer.

"I cooked this for her, Grandmother. My mother should serve it." Vivian Baxter agreed and slid the dessert over to me. Guy asked, "Is it good, is it good? I made it myself."

I had not tasted one bite, but I answered, "My son, this is the best bread pudding in the world."

It was true then, and even as you read about it today it is still the best bread pudding in the world.

BREAD PUDDING ∽

Serves 6

50g/2oz/¼ cup (½ stick) butter

1 loaf stale sliced white bread

65g/2½oz/½ cup sultanas (golden
  raisins)

200g/7oz/1 cup caster sugar

3 large eggs, beaten

475ml/16fl oz/2 cups milk

2 tablespoons vanilla extract

1 teaspoon ground cinnamon

Preheat oven to 180°C/350°F/Gas Mark 4. Grease with butter 2.8 litre/5 pint/12½ cups (3-quart) ovenproof casserole dish.

Butter both sides of bread slices, place on foil, and put into oven. Toast slices on both sides.

Place sultanas in bowl of hot water to plump up. Cover, soak for 20 minutes, and drain. Combine sugar, eggs, milk, vanilla extract and cinnamon. Mix well.

Break up toasted bread, and put in casserole dish. Add drained sultanas. Pour egg mixture over bread, and stir.

Bake 40 minutes. Serve hot or cold.

MY BIG BROTHER'S SAVINGS ACCOUNT

My ten-year-old son had a huge appetite and I had a very slim wallet. We lived in a small two-room apartment in a San Francisco Victorian. Our building provided cooking privileges for all tenants in a large kitchen down the hall.

I adored my brother, Bailey, and he was coming for dinner. I wanted to delight him by creating a new recipe. I would at the same time satisfy my always-hungry son.

Bailey was two years older than I and seven inches shorter, but he made it very clear all my life that he was my big brother. He was a good cook, and occasionally brilliance would overtake him at the stove and his culinary efforts would bedazzle. Our mother, who was the best and most adventurous cook in our family, encouraged us to be daring in creating recipes and bold in competing with each other.

I couldn't afford the ham Bailey loved, so I bought three smoked pork chops instead, which I planned to sauté and then bake with cooked apples, pineapples, and brown sugar, and I would serve braised cabbage with ginger as a side dish. I had just placed the pork chops in the skillet over a medium fire when the doorbell rang.

Bailey entered carrying a shopping bag. He was early and full of laughter. He said, "I brought dinner and I'm going to cook it." I said, "Well, I was going to cook pork chops and cabbage." He laughed and said, "Look in the shopping bag."

I emptied the contents onto the counter. There were three fresh pork chops, a head of cabbage, a green bell pepper, and a pound of bacon. He said, "I presume you have milk and another skillet."

I said, "Yes."

He said, "Let's cook together. I'm going to make a dish that will feed you and Guy for a week." He used half of the stove and I the other, and we shared a bottle of Mateus rosé wine for the next hour. He asked me to cook the rice since I make no-fail rice, and he expected that we would finish our dishes at the same time.

My son's eyes enlarged when he looked at the food-loaded table. My pork chops with the apple and pineapple were on one platter. Bailey's pork chops with bacon and a cream sauce were on the other. The molded rice towered in the middle of the table. I had served gingered cabbage and Bailey had made cabbage with celery and water chestnuts.

As he opened the door to leave, Bailey said, "Split one pork chop down to the bone, serve it with gravy, a piece of bacon, and rice – that would be one dinner. The next night serve just bacon and gravy and rice with a salad. There's another meal. Wait a couple of days and use another half pork chop, serve with spinach, rice, and gravy, or make some great biscuits, and that will be yet another dinner. Make a green salad in between. Do that and you'll be okay for a week."

As he started down the steps, he said, "If I had a million dollars, you would never have to wonder how you were going to feed my nephew. Since I don't have even a thousand dollars, a big brother can teach his little sister how she can save pennies and still keep her little crumb crusher from starving."

I shouted, "He is not a crumb crusher."

Bailey laughed and started around the building. I was yelling at the night air.

BAILEY'S SMOTHERED PORK CHOPS ∽

Serves 6

6 thick rashers back bacon

1 large Spanish onion, sliced

6 end loin pork chops

Salt and freshly ground black pepper, to taste

115g/4oz/1 cup plain (all-purpose) flour

2 tablespoons vegetable oil, if needed

250ml/8fl oz/1 cup hot water

250ml/8fl oz/1 cup milk

Fry bacon in large skillet on medium heat, and remove to paper towels to drain.

Sauté onion in same skillet with bacon fat, and remove to paper towels to drain.

Season pork chops with salt and pepper, and dredge in flour. Fry on medium heat in the same skillet with bacon fat until light brown, and remove to warm plate.

Put remaining flour into skillet (add oil if necessary). Brown flour lightly. Add hot water immediately, and then milk. Stir vigorously. Season as desired with more salt and pepper.

Put pork chops, bacon, and onion into gravy, and reduce heat to simmer. Cover skillet, and simmer for 20 minutes.

Check gravy for seasoning. Adjust as needed while food is still hot.

SMOKED PORK CHOPS ∽

Serves 3 to 5

1 tablespoon vegetable oil

3 large smoked pork chops or 3 large
    standard (unsmoked) pork chops

1 litre/1¾ pints/4 cups (1 quart) hot
    water

15g/½oz/1 tablespoon butter

2 Granny Smith apples, peeled, cored
    and diced

225g/8oz can crushed pineapple,
    drained

1 tablespoon brown sugar

⅛ teaspoon ground cinnamon

⅛ teaspoon freshly grated nutmeg

25ml/1fl oz/⅛ cup water

Preheat oven to 180°C/350°F/Gas Mark 4.

Place oil and chops in large, deep skillet, and pour hot water over chops. Simmer for 20 minutes, turning chops twice while water is simmering. Take skillet off heat. Remove chops from water, and discard water. Pat chops dry.

Place butter in small pan, and add apples. Sauté apples until they are tender. Add pineapple, brown sugar, cinnamon and nutmeg, and cook until all liquid has disappeared.

Put chops in an accommodating ovenproof dish. Cover with apple-pineapple mixture. Pour water into bottom of dish, and cover. Bake for 30 minutes. Remove lid and continue baking for 20 minutes.

BRAISED CABBAGE WITH GINGER

Serves 4

1 medium to large head of cabbage

25g/1oz/2 tablespoons (¼ stick)
   butter

½ onion, chopped

2 tablespoons peeled, grated fresh
   root ginger

1 large green (bell) pepper, seeded
   and chopped

250ml/8fl oz/1 cup chicken bouillon
   or chicken stock

Salt and freshly ground black
   pepper, to taste

Quarter cabbage, remove stalk, and cover with boiling water. Let sit for 10 minutes. Drain cabbage, and pat dry in a towel. Remove to chopping board, and cut into bite-size pieces.

Melt butter in pan over moderate heat and add cabbage, onion, ginger, green pepper and bouillon. Sauté until tender but not brown. Cover and cook over medium heat for a further 20 minutes. Season with salt and pepper. Serve at once.

CABBAGE WITH CELERY AND WATER CHESTNUTS ∽

Serves 4 to 6

1 large onion, sliced

1 green (bell) pepper, seeded and cut
into large pieces

3 sticks celery, chopped

2 tablespoons vegetable oil

1 head cabbage, cut into large
bite-size pieces

250ml/8fl oz/1 cup water

225g/8oz can water chestnut slices,
drained

Salt and freshly ground black pepper,
to taste

Sauté onion, green pepper and celery in oil until translucent but not brown. Add cabbage and water, cover and simmer for 25 to 30 minutes. Add water chestnut slices to cabbage. Season with salt and pepper. Cook 10 more minutes, and serve.

SHORT RIBS À LA
THE BIG EASY

C an you cook Creole?"
  I looked at the woman and gave her a lie as soft as melting
  butter. "Yes, of course. That's all I know how to cook."
The Creole Café had a cardboard sign in the window that announced, cook wanted. seventy-five dollars a week. As soon as I saw it I knew I could cook Creole, whatever that was.

Desperation to find help must have blinded the proprietress to my age, or perhaps it was the fact that I was six feet and had an attitude that belied my seventeen years. She didn't question me about recipes and menus, but her long brown face did trail down in wrinkles, and doubt hung on the edges of her questions.

"Can you start on Monday?"

"I'll be glad to."

"You know it's six days a week. We're closed on Sunday."

"That's fine with me. I like to go to church on Sunday." It's awful to think that the devil gave me that lie, but it came unexpectedly and worked like dollar bills. Suspicion and doubt fled from her face, and she smiled. Her teeth were all the same size, a small white picket fence semicircled in her mouth.

"Well, I know we're going to get along. You're a good Christian. I like that. Yes, ma'am, I sure do."

My need for a job stiffed my telling (confessing to) her that I mean to be a Christian but that I blow it every day. Instead, I asked her, "What time on Monday? Bless the Lord!"

"You get here at five."

Five in the morning. Those mean streets menaced by thugs who had not yet gone to sleep, pillowing on someone else's dreams. Five! Just when the streetcars began to rattle, their lighted insides looking like exclusive houses in the fog. Five!

"All right, I'll be here at five, Monday morning."

"You'll cook the dinners and put them on the steam table. You don't have to do short orders. I do that."

Mrs. Dupree was a short, plump woman of about fifty. Her hair was naturally straight and heavy. Probably Cajun, Indian, African, and white, and, naturally, Negro.

"And what's your name?"

"Rita." Marguerite was too solemn and Maya too fancy. Rita sounded like dark, flashing eyes, hot peppers, and Creole evenings with strummed guitars. "Rita Johnson."

"That's a right nice name." Then, as some people do to show their sense of familiarity, she immediately narrowed the name down. "I'll call you Reet. Okay?"

Okay, of course. I had a job. Seventy-five dollars a week. So I was Reet. Reet, poteet, and gone. All Reet. Now all I had to do was learn to cook. I asked old Papa Ford to teach me.

He had been a grown man when the twentieth century was born and left a large family of brothers and sisters in Terre Haute, Indiana (always called the East Coast), to find what the world had in store for a "good-looking colored boy with no education in his head, but a pile of larceny in his heart." He traveled with circuses "shoveling elephant shit." He shot dice in freight trains and played poker in back rooms and shanties all over the northern states. He worked as a chef on Pullman dining cars and was a fry cook in the Merchant Marine Corps.

By 1943, when I first saw him at my mother's house in San Francisco, his good looks were as delicate as an old man's memory, and disappointment rode his face bareback. His hands had gone. His gambler's fingers had thickened. During the Depression he worked at the only straight job he knew, which was carpentering. That had further toughened his "moneymakers." Mother rescued him from a job as a sweeper in a pinochle parlor and brought him home to look after the house and five roomers who rented from us.

He sorted and counted the linen when the laundry truck picked it up and returned it, then grudgingly handed out fresh sheets to the roomers. He cooked massive and delicious dinners when Mother was busy, and he sat in the tall-ceiling kitchen drinking coffee by the potfuls.

Papa Ford loved my mother (as did nearly everyone) with a childlike devotion. He went so far as to control his profanity when she was around, knowing she couldn't abide cursing unless she was doing the cursing.

When I told him I had a job as a cook and needed his help, he said, "Why the sheeit do you want to work in a goddamn kitchen washing dishes?"

"Papa, the job pays seventy-five dollars a week and I'll be cooking, not washing dishes."

"Colored women been cooking so long, thought you'd be tired of it by now."

"If you'll just tell me how to cook a few dishes …"

"High school and all that education. How come you don't get a goddamn job where you can go to work looking like something?"

I tried another tack. "I probably couldn't learn to cook Creole food anyway. It's too complicated."

"Sheeit. Ain't nothing but onions, celery, green peppers, garlic, and tomatoes. Put that in everything and you got Creole food. I already told you how to cook rice."

"Yes." I could cook rice till each grain stood separately.

"That's all, then. Them geechees can't live without swamp seed." He crackled at his joke, then recalled with a frown, "Still don't like you working as a goddamn cook. Get married. Then you don't have to cook for nobody but your own family. Sheeit.

Yeah, don't forget, put red chili pepper in everything. They'll be expecting it."

The Creole Café steamed with onion vapor, garlic mists, tomato fogs, and green pepper sprays. I put the Creole flavors into Vivian Baxter's recipe for short ribs of beef, and Salisbury steak was just hamburger with a Creole sauce.

Mrs. Dupree chose the daily menu and left a note on the steam table informing me of her gastronomic decisions. But I, Rita, the chef, decided how much garlic and how many bay leaves would flavor the steamed Shreveport tripe. For over a month I was embroiled in the mysteries of the kitchen with the expectancy of an alchemist about to discover the secret properties of gold.

Only after the mystery had worn down to a layer of commonness did I begin to notice the customers. They consisted largely of light-skinned, slick-haired Creoles from Louisiana, who spoke French patois only a little less complicated than the contents of my pots and equally spicy. I thought it fitting and not at all unusual that they enjoyed my cooking. I was following Papa Ford's instructions loosely and adding artistic touches of my own. Mrs. Dupree said I was building up her business.

Our customers never just ate, paid, and left. They sat for hours on the long backless stools and exchanged gossip or shared the patient philosophy of the black South.

Near the steam counter, the soft sounds of black talk, the sharp reports of laughter, and the shuffling feet on tiled floors mixed themselves in odorous vapors. I was content. My cooking was appreciated. I had pockets full of money and my son was well looked after. I may not have been happy. I was content.

BRAISED SHORT RIBS OF BEEF ⌒

Serves 8

2.25kg/5lb beef short ribs, cut into
7.5cm/3in pieces

Salt and freshly ground black pepper,
to taste

½ teaspoon meat tenderizer

Plain (all-purpose) flour, for sprinkling

2 tablespoons vegetable oil

750ml/1¼ pints/3 cups meat stock or
water

5 medium carrots, peeled and cut into
4cm/1½in pieces

Two 400g/14oz cans tomatoes

175g/6oz can tomato puree (paste)

2 large onions, diced

3 sticks celery, chopped

3 cloves garlic, diced

2 green (bell) peppers, seeded and
cut into large pieces

2 bay leaves

250ml/8fl oz/1 cup good cabernet
sauvignon

1 tablespoon chopped fresh parsley

Preheat oven to 180°C/350°F/Gas Mark 4.

Season meat with salt and pepper, sprinkle with meat tenderizer, and dust with flour. (I sprinkle meat tenderizer on all meat, since I expect it to be tough.) Brown on all sides in oil in large flameproof casserole dish. Add stock; cover and bake in the oven for 1 hour.

Remove from oven and add carrots, tomatoes, tomato puree, onions, celery, garlic, green peppers, bay leaves and wine. Return to oven, and cook 1½ hours. Meat should be very tender. Remove bay leaves, and adjust seasoning as needed.

On large serving dish, arrange vegetables around meat, and sprinkle with chopped parsley.

MOTHER'S LONG VIEW

Independence is a heady draft, and if you drink it in your youth it can have the same effect on the brain as young wine. It does not matter that its taste is not very appealing; it is addictive and with each drink the consumer wants more.

When I was twenty and living in San Francisco, I had a three-year-old son, two jobs, and two rented rooms with cooking privileges down the hall. My landlady, Mrs. Jefferson, was kind and grandmotherly. She was a ready babysitter and insisted on providing dinner for her tenants. Her ways were so tender and her personality so sweet that no one was mean enough to discourage her disastrous culinary exploits. Spaghetti at her table, which was offered at least three times a week, was a mysterious red, white, and brown concoction. We would occasionally encounter an unidentifiable piece of meat floating on the plate.

There was no money in my budget to afford restaurant food, so my son and I were often loyal, if unhappy, diners at Chez Jefferson.

My mother had moved from Post Street into a fourteen-room Victorian house on Fulton Street, which she had filled with gothic, heavily carved furniture. The upholstery on the sofa and occasional chairs was red-wine-colored mohair. Oriental rugs were placed throughout the house. She had a live-in employee who was a fill-in cook for her and cleaned the house.

Mother picked up Guy two or three times a week and took him

to her house where she fed him peaches and cream and hot dogs, but I only went to her house when she was expecting me.

My mother understood and encouraged my self-reliance. We had a standing appointment, which I looked forward to eagerly. Once a month, she would cook one of my favorite dishes and I would go to her house for lunch. One important date that stands out in my mind I call Vivian's Red Rice Day.

When I arrived at the Fulton Street house my mother was dressed beautifully, her makeup was perfect, and she wore good jewelry.

After we embraced, I washed my hands and we walked through her formal dark dining room and into the large bright kitchen.

Much of lunch was already on the table. Vivian Baxter cooked wonderful meals and was very serious about how to present them.

On that long-ago Red Rice Day, my mother had placed on the table a dry, crispy, roasted capon, no dressing or gravy, and a simple lettuce salad, no tomatoes or cucumbers. A widemouthed bowl covered with a platter sat next to her plate.

She blessed the table with a fervent but brief prayer and put her left hand on the platter and her right on the bowl and turned the dishes over. She gently loosened the bowl from its contents and revealed a tall mound of glistening red rice (my favorite food in all the world) decorated with finely minced parsley and the green tops of scallions.

The chicken and salad do not feature so prominently on my taste buds' memory, but each grain of red rice is emblazoned on the surface of my tongue forever.

Gluttonous and greedy negatively describe the hearty eater offered the seduction of her favorite food.

Two large portions of rice sated my appetite, but the deliciousness of the dish made me long for a larger stomach so that I could eat two more helpings.

My mother had plans for the rest of the afternoon, so she gathered her wraps and we left the house together.

We reached the middle of the block and were enveloped in the stinging acid aroma of vinegar from the pickle factory on the corner of Fillmore and Fulton streets. I had walked ahead. My mother stopped me and said, "Baby."

I walked back to her.

"Baby. I've been thinking and now I am sure. You are the greatest woman I've ever met."

My mother was five feet four inches to my six-foot frame.

I looked down at the pretty little woman, and her perfect makeup and diamond earrings, who owned a hotel and was admired by most people in San Francisco's black community.

She continued, "You are very kind and very intelligent and those elements are not always found together. Mrs. Eleanor Roosevelt, Dr. Mary McLeod Bethune, and my mother – yes, you belong in that category. Here, give me a kiss."

She kissed me on the lips and turned and jaywalked across the street to her beige and brown Pontiac. I pulled myself together and walked down to Fillmore Street. I crossed there and waited for the number 22 streetcar.

My policy of independence would not allow me to accept money or even a ride from my mother, but I welcomed her wisdom. Now I thought of her statement. I thought, Suppose she is right. She's very intelligent and she often said she didn't fear anyone enough to lie to him, so suppose she is right. Imagine, I really might be somebody. Imagine.

At that moment, when I could still taste the red rice, I decided the time had come when I should cut down on dangerous habits like smoking, drinking, and cursing.

Imagine, I might really become somebody.

RED RICE ∽

Serves 8

225g/8oz thick back bacon rashers
2 medium onions, chopped
1 small red (bell) pepper, seeded and
    chopped
475ml/16fl oz/2 cups canned
    chopped tomatoes
175g/6oz can tomato puree (paste)
Pinch of freshly ground black pepper
½ teaspoon salt
450g/1lb/4 cups cooked white rice
475ml/16fl oz/2 cups water

Fry bacon in a large skillet on medium heat until brown, stirring with fork. Add onions and red pepper. Cover and cook for 2 to 3 minutes. Remove lid and add remaining ingredients; mix well. Bring to boil, about 3 minutes. Stir vigorously, cover again, and cook over very low heat for about 15 minutes until rice and liquid are totally mixed.

ROASTED CAPON ∽

Serves 4

900g–1.3kg/2–3lb capon or chicken
Juice of 1 lemon
250ml/8fl oz/1 cup water
50g/2oz/¼ cup (½ stick) butter
Salt and freshly ground black pepper,
    to taste
1 unpeeled Granny Smith apple,
    cored and cut into pieces
1 stick celery, cut into pieces

Preheat oven to 180°C/350°F/Gas Mark 4.

Wash capon in lemon juice mixed with water. Pat dry, and rub butter over bird. Liberally salt and pepper bird outside and inside. Place apple and celery in capon cavity.

Make foil tent, and place over bird. Bake for 1 hour, periodically basting with juices in pan. Remove foil. Reduce oven to 160°C/325°F/Gas Mark 3 and bake for 30 more minutes.

GOOD BANANA,
BAD TIMING

T. R. Mansfield was short and mean and lean. He was mostly bones, with no spare meat anywhere on his body. His lemon-colored skin was pockmarked as a result of childhood chicken pox. He was literate, but just barely.

I was nineteen years old and crazy for him. When I was not occupied fulfilling my duties as a short-order cook or selling jazz music in a record store, I thought of nothing but T.R. Maybe it was his way of walking that captured and held me. He moved as if his chest and upper torso had no connection with the rest of his body and was pleased at the arrangement. Which meant that his hips swung with a giant promise of better things to come.

Or maybe it was his silence that intrigued me.

I had lived with or around my mother and brother who talked all the time. They could, at no notice at all, hold conversations on the Soviet Union, the Supreme Court, race relations, or whether salmon croquettes could adequately compete with fried pork chops.

I cannot remember T.R. ever initiating a discussion, and his rejoinders to my attempts to start a conversation were generally met with a throat clearing:

"Ah-hum. Great."

Or:

"Ah-hum-rum. Yeah."

Or:

"Ah-hum-rum. No."

I visited him in his rented room twice a week and always left happier and more at peace than when I arrived. I thought he was equally pleased. Of course with his inveterate silence, I could not be expected to know otherwise.

One evening, however, when I knocked at his door, a woman answered. I stood in amazement as the door opened and a short, very plain, light-skinned, plump woman twenty years my senior said, "Come in. You must be Maya."

I walked into the room and remained silent. The woman continued, "We must have gotten our days mixed up. You usually come on Tuesdays and Fridays. I come on Mondays, Wednesdays, and Saturdays. What's today?" She looked at her watch. "Ooo, I'm running late. T.R. is in the bathroom. Well, we probably won't see each other again. Bye-bye."

My brain was in shock; there was a straitjacket around my body. I didn't think. I couldn't move.

T.R. came out of the bathroom, surprised to see me. He grumbled low, "What are you doing here?"

I could comprehend, but I still couldn't speak.

"You not due today. Today is for Daphne. She let you in?"

He had never said that much to me in our nine-month relationship.

"Come on in the kitchen." I followed him down the hall. He took a dessert from the refrigerator and placed large spoonfuls on two plates.

"Get a fork." He nodded toward a drawer and began to eat with the serving spoon. He was hard to understand at best, and now with his mouth full of bananas and custard and vanilla wafers I should not have understood a word. But I will never forget what he said or its impact on me.

"Daphne. Ever hear of a Negro woman named Daphne? She makes this for me once a month. Her grandmother was a white woman."

Everybody I knew had at least one white grandparent or great grandparent. No one thought it was something to brag about.

"I've been loving her a long time. She's too good for me and she's married, but she comes anyway. You look all stove up like you're mad. Wait now, I never promised you anything and I'm going to be with Daphne as long as she'll have me. So just wipe that stupid look off your face."

He had finished his pudding and was digging for more. I looked at the sweet. The custard was poorly made and was already weeping pure water, the bananas were brown from exposure, and the vanilla wafers were soggy. Then I looked at T.R. He was a slothful, ignorant, and arrogant fool.

I stood up and pushed my plate to him and walked out.

On the street, I realized I had not said one word from the moment I entered that house until I left.

I stopped at the supermarket on the way home. In my kitchen I began to make my own banana pudding. When it was finished and properly chilled, my son and I sat down and ate it.

Poor T.R., he never had – and now never would have – a chance to taste a truly great banana pudding. I ate his portion that night and with each morsel I knew I would never see him again.

BANANA PUDDING ∽

Serves 8

150g/5oz/¾ cup caster sugar, plus
   1 tablespoon caster sugar
40g/1½oz/⅓ cup cornflour (cornstarch)
Pinch of salt
750ml/1¼ pints/3 cups milk
8 eggs, separated
40g/1½oz/3 tablespoons butter
1 tablespoon vanilla extract
250g/9oz/3 cups vanilla wafer cookies
4 ripe bananas, thinly sliced
½ teaspoon cream of tartar

Preheat oven to 180°C/350°F/Gas Mark 4.

Combine 65g/2½oz/⅓ cup sugar, the cornflour and salt in a large saucepan; stir until blended. Stir in milk. Cook over medium heat, stirring constantly until thickened and boiling; boil 1 minute, then remove from heat.

In small bowl, whisk egg yolks, then whisk in about 120ml/4fl oz/½ cup of the hot custard until blended. Pour yolk mixture back into custard in saucepan; cook over medium heat, stirring, for 2 minutes. Stir in butter and vanilla until blended.

Place half the vanilla wafers on bottom of shallow 2 litre/3½ pint/8 cup (2 quart) ovenproof casserole dish. Top with layers of banana slices and custard. Repeat layering, ending with custard.

Whisk egg whites and 50g/2oz/¼ cup sugar in large mixing bowl at low speed until frothy. Add cream of tartar; increase speed to medium and gradually whisk in remaining sugar. Whisk until whites just hold stiff peaks.

Immediately spoon meringue over hot custard, being sure that meringue touches baking dish on all sides (this helps prevent it from shrinking). Transfer to oven and bake until golden, about 20 minutes. Remove from oven and cool 1 hour. Refrigerate at least 4 hours before serving.

READY-TO-WEAR TRIPE

My friend Sam Floyd was the most dapper, eloquently dressing man I ever knew. Had he lived during the flapper days, he would have been one of the first to wear spats. In another age, he would have sported a foulard or a four-in-hand. He certainly would have owned a derby and a fedora. In fact, somewhere in his crowded closet in his crowded apartment in New York's Greenwich Village, he did have a beret from Paris and a top hat for formal evenings out on the New York town.

In the 1960s, he wore Brooks Brothers suits, Van Huesen shirts, and Sulka silk ties. His shoes were custom-made.

In 1969, Sam and I flew out to California to visit my mother, who was the most elegant-dressing woman I ever knew. She wore Daché hats and Lilli Ann suits, Lillie Rubin dresses, and Daniel Green slippers. They admired and even liked each other. They were a match.

Sam and I were invited to dinner by a friend of my mother's, who declined to go. The date started to go bad from the first minute. Our host opened the door and invited us directly to the bar in his den. He told Sam that he shouldn't have dressed up. He added, "There's no one in my house you have to impress."

I knew he was being friendly. Sam was offended. Sam wouldn't have thought that what he was wearing was dress-up. He said, "I didn't really have to try to achieve this just to come to your house."

I knew Sam was just being Sam, but now the host was offended. Just as he was preparing his rejoinder, I stepped in.

"May we order drinks? I've got dust in my throat." That was the height of the evening.

In a half hour, the host had stopped speaking to Sam who retaliated by trying to drink the bar dry. Sam ordinarily drank one or two whiskeys before dinner and some wine with the meal. On that particular night, Sam had whiskey after whiskey, and when dinner was served he refused the wine, saying he would go out with whom he came in. He ordered another scotch.

I don't think he tasted the food, and as quickly as I could, still being courteous, I said our thanks and good-byes.

Just before he passed out in my car, Sam said, "I drank because that jerk bored me."

He lurched into my mother's house and straight into the guest room. In the morning I was having coffee when he came into the kitchen holding his head.

"I drank everything I could to get back at our host."

I said, "And he's feeling it this morning, poor thing."

Sam said, "Don't add insult to injury."

Mother entered, saying, "Only if it is deserved."

I looked at both people whom I loved and thought how much alike they were. They were separated by a generation and by gender, but at 9:00 a.m. both had showered and chosen expensive dressing gowns just to come to the kitchen.

I asked Sam to recount for my mother what he could remember of the night before. I headed back to my room. When I returned, my mother was laughing heartily.

"What you need is a cold beer now, and as soon as I can make it, some tripe. Some good red-hot tripe and white rice! Or I can make the Mexican menudo."

Sam said, "I only know how to cook tripe à la mode de Caen." He pronounced the dish with a French accent.

My mother asked, "What?"

He started to tell her.

She said, "Wait, let me change. I'll be right back, and I'll cook my kind of tripe and you can tell me your recipe."

She went back to her room. Sam took his beer and disappeared, and I returned to my room.

I smelled onions frying and I followed the aroma to the kitchen. My mother, dressed in white, was stirring onions in a skillet.

Within minutes Sam entered, also in white. They looked at each other and laughed.

Sam said, "The beer saved my life. I'll have another."

Mother said, "Why don't you make us a few dry martinis? We'll eat soon."

I asked, "You cooked tripe that fast?"

"I used my pressure cooker, but it doesn't take as long as it used to now that they process tripe. They clean it and then precook it."

We sat at the table suffused in delicious aroma. Suddenly Sam's sleeve was caught on the martini glass and it tipped into his plate of tripe; then his plate slipped over onto my mother's lap. We all jumped. Sam apologized. Mother went to the sink.

I said, "Let's go to your bathroom and get some water on it immediately." We rushed to her room. When she had immersed her slacks and shirt in the basin she chose another white set and we walked back into the kitchen.

Sam Floyd had cleaned the table and put on a fresh tablecloth. We all had new plates.

Sam said, "I'm rarely clumsy enough to ruin someone else's clothes. And on only one other occasion have I spilled tomato sauce on my own self."

We sat down and enjoyed the food. Mother said, "This is good hangover food. Never fails."

Just as we finished eating, Sam tipped his plate. Red sauce spilled onto his summer white outfit.

My mother said, "You clever thing, you did that on purpose."

Sam swore he didn't plan to pour tripe on his clothes and maybe he didn't, but I know with that accident he made my mother his friend for life.

TRIPE À LA MODE DE CAEN ∞

Serves 4 to 6

900g/2lb fresh tripe

Bouquet Garni (p. 9)

3 carrots, peeled and diced

3 Spanish onions, diced

2 sticks celery, diced

3 cloves garlic, diced

115g/4oz diced salt pork, cut into
  large pieces

4 bay leaves

10 black peppercorns

1 pig's foot

1 pork soup bone, cracked

1 teaspoon salt

250ml/8fl oz/1 cup water

475ml/16fl oz/2 cups dry white wine

2 jiggers (two 40ml/1½fl oz) gin

Preheat oven to 180°C/350°F/Gas Mark 4.

Wash tripe, and cut into bite-size cubes. Put all dry ingredients into large ovenproof earthenware dish. Pour in water, wine and gin. Cover tightly and bake for 5 hours. Remove from oven, and discard pig's foot, soup bone and Bouquet Garni. Serve with crusty French bread.

RED TRIPE WITH WHITE RICE ∞

Serves 4 to 6

900g/2lb fresh tripe

2 tablespoons vegetable oil

1 small onion, sliced

Four 400g/14oz cans tomatoes

175g/6oz can tomato puree (paste)

2 cloves garlic, minced

Salt and freshly ground black pepper,
   to taste

Dried red pepper or chilli flakes,
   to taste

450–675g/1–1½lb/4–6 cups hot
   cooked white rice

Wash tripe and cut into 2.5cm/1in pieces. Put in saucepan with water to cover, and simmer for 1½ hours. Drain, and pat dry.

In large skillet, sauté oil, onion, tomatoes, tomato puree and garlic. Add tripe. Simmer 1 hour, or until tender. Season with salt, pepper and dried red pepper flakes. Serve with rice.

MENUDOS (TRIPE STEW) ∽

Serves 8

2.25kg/5lb fresh tripe

1 large beef soup bone

4 cloves garlic, chopped

3 teaspoons salt

4 medium onions, chopped

1 teaspoon ground coriander

2 tablespoons chilli powder (or more,
    to taste) or 115g/4oz can chopped
    green chillies

1.5 litres/2½ pints/6¼ cups
    (1½ quarts) water

Two 400g/14oz cans whole hominy
    (hulled maize/corn)

Juice of 1 lemon

1 tablespoon chopped fresh
    coriander (cilantro)

Wash tripe, and cut into 1cm/½in wide strips.

Place tripe, soup bone, garlic, salt, onions, ground coriander, chilli powder and water in a large saucepan. Simmer for 6 hours, or until tripe is tender, adding more water if necessary. Add hominy, lemon juice and chopped coriander, and cook over medium to high heat for 30 minutes. Remove soup bone, and serve immediately.

M.J. AND THE DOCTOR AND MEXICAN FOOD

The handsome doctor cared inordinately for tamales, and my friend-sister, the beautiful Mary Jane, called M.J., cared for the doctor. He had been the senior surgeon when Mary Jane was taken into a hospital with a life-threatening emergency. In hours, following the diligent application of his medical know-how, her life was saved and her principal savior was a handsome, young, dashing, unmarried doctor.

She returned home and used gargantuan control to keep herself from calling the doctor. Much to her delight, after a week he telephoned her and telephoned her and telephoned her until she agreed to go out with him. The courtship started slow and remained slow. The doctor was steady, but his ardor never heated up to the degree that M.J. wanted so that she could know the level of his commitment.

One day she invited me to visit. She lived in Santa Monica on the ground floor in a generous apartment of a building she owned. Her living room was rich with antique furniture, and the paintings of John Biggers, Elizabeth Catlett, and Samella Lewis hung on her walls.

M.J. was a rich-cream-colored woman with green-gray eyes and an electric personality. She told me that the doctor was coming for dinner and that she had an incredible recipe for tamales. Her smile of satisfaction was just comfortably one grin away from a smirk.

When I probed, she said her suitor loved Mexican food and he thought only some California Mexicans and a few Texas Mexicans could prepare tamales properly. She said whenever he was near a Mexican restaurant that served tamales, he was like a runaway horse. She had seen him pull up and halt and all but paw the ground at its door.

M.J. had bought all the ingredients to make dozens of her beloved's delight. She knew I cooked Mexican food often and she wanted me to see that everything went off well. I sat on a kitchen stool as she made arroz con pollo, refried beans, guacamole, salsa, carne Colorado, and, finally, the vaunted tamales. Her entire house was filled with the culinary perfumes of Guadalajara and Oaxaca and Jalisco.

The doctor entered the living room, but when we were introduced he could hardly concentrate enough to complete the simplest social pleasantries of "How are you?" and "Well, and you?"

I watched as his nostrils twitched from side to side, trying to ascertain if the aromas he thought he encountered were really there. He asked M.J. if she had sent out for Mexican food. She told him she had cooked the dinner. He asked what was on the menu. She answered, "Guacamole, chips, salsa, arroz con pollo," and so forth. She listed all the dishes except the much-adored tamales.

With each mention of food his smile widened and his body seemed to wave. He said, "If you had told me, I could have picked up some tamales. I was near the café."

She said, "Maybe we'll make do tonight. Maya is eating with us. Will you make drinks?"

The doctor surprised me. He was familiar enough with M.J.'s house to know where the liquor was kept and where to find highball glasses. She had not told me everything.

M.J. had set the table with colorful linens and Mexican plates. When she served the beans and rice, the carne Colorado, and the chicken and rice, the doctor spoke from the depth of a deep enchantment. "You made this? You yourself?"

As she headed toward the kitchen, she motioned me to sit down. I did so.

"Who would have thought that a smart and pretty woman like you could cook like this? This table looks like the real thing. If you had told me, I could have picked up some tamales."

She walked in carrying a plate filled with the doctor's dream comestibles. When he saw the platter he lost all sense of propriety. He plucked a tamale and put it on his plate. When he unwrapped the hot savory from the cornhusks, his face was a study in hope and apprehension. The long cornmeal tamale lay on his plate, and he waited a few seconds just in case it wasn't as good as he wished. Then he lifted his fork and cut a bite and put it in his mouth.

As the flavored cornmeal and the seasoned meat filling melted, he began to smile. Then the smile widened and he started to laugh. He made no eye contact, so he wasn't sharing the laughter. He was just enjoying himself with himself. When he finished the tamale, he looked at M.J. Looked at her as if he had never really seen her. Looked at her and realized that this woman who pleased him in many other ways could also cook tamales to make his heart stand still.

I was not at all surprised when M.J. told me that later that night he said he wanted to talk about a longtime commitment.

TAMALES DE MAIZ CON POLLO ✌

(green cornhusk tamales with chicken filling)

Makes 1 dozen tamales*

2 whole chicken breasts

2 tablespoons vegetable oil

1 medium onion, minced

2 cloves garlic, minced

15g/½oz/¼ cup chopped fresh parsley

25g/1oz/½ cup chopped fresh
    coriander (cilantro)

¼ teaspoon cayenne pepper

1 teaspoon salt

Freshly ground black pepper, to taste

200g/7oz/1¾ cups masa, cornmeal or
    coarse polenta

250ml/8fl oz/1 cup warm water

40g/1½oz/¼ cup lard

24 fresh cornhusks

Wash chicken breasts, and cut from bone. Slice chicken into pencil-thin strips.

In large sauté pan, sauté chicken in oil for 15 minutes, or until done, and then remove from oil.

Sauté onion and garlic in oil until translucent. Return chicken to sauté pan, and add parsley, coriander, cayenne pepper and ½ teaspoon salt, and season with black pepper. Set aside to cool.

In heavy-based saucepan, mix together masa, water, remaining salt and lard, and stir and cook over medium heat until very creamy and smooth, about 20 to 25 minutes. Cool to room temperature.

Trim the thick bottom part from cornhusks and wash well, removing any silk. For each tamale, take 2 cornhusks, pointed part at top, and paste together at one side with some of the masa mixture. This makes the husk wider. Now spread 1 tablespoon of the masa mixture on the inside about 2.5cm/1in from the bottom and extending about 5cm/2in up the husk. Top with 2 teaspoons of the chicken filling. Fold husk around filling, paste with a little more masa, and then fold bottom towards top, making envelopes. Tie together with kitchen string.

Stand up in a steamer, and steam for 1 hour.

* Tamales may be frozen and reheated
  over steam.

SAVING FACE AND SMOKING
IN ITALY

The Rockefeller Foundation's Study and Conference Center was a large mansion snuggled into the hills above Bellagio, Italy. Fifteen artists at a time from around the world were invited to the enclave. Selected artists with companions had to make their way to Milan airport, and then magically they were swept up by tender arms and placed in a lap of luxury that few popular movie stars or rich corporate chiefs even dreamed existed. A chauffeured car picked up the invitees and drove them carefully fifty miles north to Bellagio. There they were deposited at the Center, which stood atop a high hill. Its buildings were low-slung and meandered over carefully tended acres only a few miles from the Swiss border. Within those elegant walls, forty-eight employees cared for thirty guests and the retreat center's director and wife. Each artist had a commodious suite.

Once ensconced in this graciousness, the artists were informed of the regimen. Breakfast was ordered nightly and served each morning by footmen. Lunch was served informally at midday. Artists could sit at will in a casual dining room and choose food from an elaborate buffet. The time could have been passed off as an ordinary lunch save that each table sported a handwritten menu of foods offered and the company was served at the buffet table by the uniformed head waiter and the tailored butler.

The artists were addressed as *dottore*, which meant that their scholarship was respected. They were told that dinner was formal, and that was an understatement. Dinner was an event of meticulous structure. Guests were expected to dress each night and were directed where to sit by a placement, which lay on a hall table at the door of the drawing room. There must have been an exemplary social statistician in the Center's employ because in the four weeks when I was a resident, no one ever sat twice between the same two people.

Jessica Mitford and I were invited and found ourselves to be the only female artists. We had brought along our husbands, Robert Treuhaft and Paul du Feu, but the staff, so unused to female scholars, could not bring themselves to address us as they addressed the thirteen male scholars. So they called us *signora* and our husbands *dottore*.

One evening during a lull in the ten or twelve conversations plying the table, the director reminded the guests that Thanksgiving was approaching. He then asked if anyone had a good recipe for roast turkey and corn bread dressing. I waited, but no one moved. I said, "I do. I have a recipe." I spoke it before I thought.

Everyone beamed at me except my husband, Jessica, and Robert. In a second, their faces told me I had done the wrong thing. Company never volunteers, never offers. Nonetheless, the director said the butler would come to my suite midmorning to collect the recipe.

I broke my writing schedule to recall and write the recipe. I handed the missive to the butler. Within minutes he returned and said the chef wanted to see the *dottore* who had sent him the recipe. I followed him down a flight of dark stairs and, without a hint of change to come, stepped suddenly into a vast, noisy, hot, brightly lit kitchen, where a fleet of white-uniformed cooks were stirring steaming pots and sizzling pans. The butler guided me over to meet the head chef, who wore a starched white toque. His surprise at seeing me let me know that he had expected Dottore Angelou to be a white male, and, instead, a six-foot-tall daughter of Africa stood before him ready to answer his questions. He did shake my hand, but he then turned his back rather rudely and shouted to another cook, "Come and talk to this woman. I don't have the time."

The second cook tried his English, but I told him we could speak Italian. He said, "Signora, we want to follow your recipe, but we have never made corn bread or corn bread dressing. We need your help."

I asked for cornmeal, only to be offered polenta. I asked for baking powder and was told they didn't even know what that was. When I described the work of baking powder, I was shown a large slab of moist yeast. The polenta was an orange powdery meal many times brighter than American yellow cornmeal.

During the Easter seasons, my mother always used yeast to make hot cross buns. I figured I could use it as the riser for my corn bread.

I gave my jacket to the butler and listed the other ingredients I needed. He put men to work, and in seconds I was able to put a pan of polenta corn bread into a hot oven and the turkey's neck, gizzard, liver, and wingtips to boil. I added celery, onions, a stick of cinnamon, and garlic to the pot.

When the bread came from the oven, hot and smoking, the head chef was standing near me. We both looked at the orange brown crust. His eyes widened. He said, "*Bella.*"

I said, "This is the bread my people eat."

The chef asked, "Who are your people?"

I answered, "African Americans. My ancestors came from Africa to America."

The chef said, "Every person in America except the Indians had ancestors who came from some other place."

I couldn't argue that.

He asked, "What makes you different from other Americans?"

I said, "My skin is black. That tells me and everyone who sees me who I am."

He raised his voice. "Roberto, Roberto, come."

A small dark-skinned cook came from the rear of the kitchen.

The chef said, "Here is Roberto. He is from Sicily, but because of his color should I call him an Afro-Italian?"

There was a burst of loud laughter. We had been speaking in Italian and everyone had heard our conversation and enjoyed the fact that the chef was putting me on.

I decided to stop the razzing and get on with the cooking. I quickly diced an onion and sautéed it in a large pan. I drained the stock and mixed some with the onion and crumbled corn bread in a large bowl. No one offered to help me, so I took the raw turkey and stuffed it with dressing. I laced the turkey's cavity and placed it into a roasting pan. I cut the oven down and set the turkey to roast.

I finely diced another onion and sautéed it and made gravy using the cut-up meat and the rest of the stock. I put a drop of the gravy on my thumb and tasted it for seasoning.

When I looked up, I realized the chef had been watching me for the past twenty minutes. His face told me he had been watching with approval.

He asked, "Would you like a smoke?"

I said, "Yes."

His nod told me to follow him. He shouted to the cooking staff, "Watch her sauce, and keep an eye on the turkey in the oven."

We walked out into an alley. He gave me a strong French cigarette and lighted his own and mine. He breathed in deeply and exhaled loudly, and although he never said a mumbling word I knew his invitation to me to join him in a smoke was his way to show his approval.

That night when the exclusive intellectual assemblage had gathered around the dining table, the chef entered followed by his sous-chef, who carried a fine brown turkey.

The sous-chef lifted the platter and bowed to the chef, who gave a small bow, then reached out his right hand to me and asked me to stand. All the scholars and their mates and the director applauded the turkey, the chef, and me.

I learned that day that a respect for food and its preparation could obliterate distances between sexes, languages, oceans, and continents.

ROASTED TURKEY ∽

Serves 15 to 20

6.8–7.8kg/15–17lb turkey

1 tablespoon salt

Corn Bread Stuffing (p. 118)

115g/4oz/½ cup (1 stick) butter,
   melted

Preheat oven to 160°C/325°F/Gas Mark 3.

Wash turkey thoroughly, and pat dry.

Rub turkey's neck and body cavities with salt. Lightly fill body cavity with Corn Bread Stuffing. Tie legs together with string. Stuff neck cavity lightly with stuffing. Draw neck skin over cavity to the back, and fasten with a skewer. Fasten wings behind back by bending tip ends under.

The turkey can be roasted in an open tin or closed roaster, or wrapped in foil. Open-tin method is preferable and is described here.

Place turkey, breast-side up, on wire rack in shallow roasting tin. Insert roasting thermometer between thigh and body, avoiding bone.

Cover bird with cheesecloth dipped in melted butter. If cheesecloth dries during cooking time, spoon some of the drippings in pan over it.

Roast until thermometer registers 88°C/190°F, or until drumsticks can be moved up and down easily. When bird is done, remove cloth. Place turkey on a large hot platter. Let stand for about 20 minutes before carving, so the meat will absorb its own juices.

CORN BREAD STUFFING ∽

Serves 8 to 10

Turkey neck

Turkey wingtip

Turkey gizzard

Turkey liver

1 teaspoon salt

3 tablespoons vegetable oil

2 sticks celery, diced

1 small onion, diced

1 quantity cooked corn bread, cooled
   (use Crackling Corn Bread recipe
   on p. 27, but omit cracklings)

4 tablespoons dried sage

1 tablespoon dried oregano

3 large eggs

Preheat oven to 180°C/350°F/Gas Mark 4. Grease a 23cm/9in square baking tin.

Place washed turkey parts in 4 litre/7 pint/16 cup (4 quart) saucepan. Add enough water to cover. Add salt, boil, and then let cool.

Into a large sauté pan, put oil, celery and onion and sauté until tender. Let cool.

Crumble corn bread, and add sage, oregano, and sautéed onion-and-celery mixture.

Strain turkey parts, reserving broth. Chop neck, gizzard, and liver meats. Pour broth and chopped meats into corn bread mixture. Add eggs, and mix well.

Add some stuffing to turkey cavity and some to neck cavity (see p. 116). Spoon rest of stuffing into prepared baking tin, and bake for 30 minutes.

HAUTE CUISINE À LA
TABASCO

M iss Annabelle Ross was a sweetly sympathetic figure. In her sixties she was prematurely old and had the manner of what southerners call a settled lady. Yet she was a coloratura soprano with *Porgy and Bess*, which meant that she was a member of a highly trained, largely young cast of opera singers who could, and did, belt out the blues just as easily as they sang bel canto Respighi, Verdi, and the art songs of Purcell.

She was not the only older singer in the group, but the others over age fifty entertained themselves by playing stud poker, keno, and cut-throat pinochle, which they called pig knuckles. They also drank their portion of gin martinis, Black & White scotch, and Jack Daniel's whiskey.

Miss Ross played no games, nor did she drink or smoke. Until she was called on stage she sat closed inside her wall of niceness looking lost and very sad. I was twenty-six years old, and because I doted on my grandmother who doted on me I had a tender feeling for older women, the grandmotherly type.

Porgy and Bess was appearing at the Teatre Wagram in Paris, and I was the principal dancer and sang the role of Ruby. I doubled singing blues and calypso in nightclubs after the curtain fell at the opera.

I watched Miss Ross and wondered how I could raise her spirits. One early evening I went to Fouquets Restaurant on the Champs Elysées. I asked to speak to the maître d'hôtel. My presence shocked him. He had not been summoned by many six-foot-tall African American girls.

He asked me in French if I had ever visited a first-class restaurant. I replied, "No, but I am young and certainly I will do so in my life."

He nodded. I told him about Miss Ross. I described her age and her loneliness. I said I didn't have much money but that I'd like to bring her to his restaurant for one great dinner. It might be her first and last time to have a superb French meal. His countenance softened and he called two waiters and repeated my story. I was invited inside to a table where the four of us sat down and pored over the menu.

The experts chose a pâté to start, then molded eggs polignac for our second course. We would be served veal medallions for our entrée. A waiter showed me my bill. I was amazed at how little I was charged. Then I realized the maître d' had reduced the price because of my story.

On the designated night, Miss Ross and I got out of a taxi. We had dressed in our best and made ourselves up to go out for a fancy Parisian evening.

We were greeted at the door as if we were royalty. Every waiter made his way by to say hello. Obviously our tale had been told to the entire staff. The maître d' seated us and within seconds there was a crowd of waiters around the table bringing still and carbonated water, serving bread and butter, and placing salt and pepper and mustard.

To my surprise, Miss Ross was a refreshing dinner guest. She told charming stories and had a ready repartee. When the meal was served, I sat at attention to observe how she would enjoy her two-star dinner.

She tasted the pâté. She said she really liked that. She had long been partial to liverwurst but preferred it on white bread with a thick slab of raw onions and lots of mayonnaise. The molded eggs polignac also delighted Miss Ross. The staff sent approving nods around the room as the veal was served because Miss Ross made a slight smacking sound and rubbed her hands together.

She tasted the meat. "Now this is good." She took another bite of the medallions. The nearest waiter recorded her approval and sent her reaction to his colleagues.

Miss Ross said, "This is close to perfect. These people can truly cook."

I was reminded of my mother's actions in restaurants. When she was particularly pleased with a dinner, she would send a glass of wine to the chef. I didn't think I had enough money for that gesture, but I was floating in self-admiration until I heard Miss Ross say, "All this needs is a little Tabasco."

I looked at her, knowing that I had to dissuade her from asking the waiter to bring her the spicy sauce. But as I turned, Miss Ross was extricating a slim bottle of Tabasco from her purse.

"This is going to make this meat right perfect. I mean perfect."

She shook the bottle over the medallions, then she closed the bottle and placed it back in her purse.

The waiters were horrified. Although stricken, at least they were able to move around the restaurant. The maître d'hôtel was so shocked, however, that he disappeared from the floor, and I confess I wanted to join him.

I have grown a little since that incident. I've come to believe that each diner should be free to flavor her dish as she wants it. For no matter how wonderfully trained the chef, no matter how delicate his or her sensitivity, taste buds are as individual as fingerprints. Mine are mine and yours are yours and *vive la différence*.

I offer you here my veal medallions recipe. BYOT (bring your own Tabasco). It's optional.

VEAL MEDALLIONS ∽

Serves 6

675g/1½lb thin veal escallops

Plain (all-purpose) flour, for sprinkling

40g/1½oz/3 tablespoons butter

1 tablespoon olive oil

Salt and freshly ground black pepper, to taste

150g/5oz/2 cups button mushrooms

250ml/8fl oz/1 cup fruity white wine

15g/½oz/¼ cup chopped fresh parsley

Dust veal with flour, and in large sauté pan brown quickly on both sides in 20g/¾oz/1½ tablespoons butter mixed with oil. Remove veal, and season with salt and pepper. Keep warm.

Sauté mushrooms until soft. Cover with 175ml/6fl oz/¾ cup wine, and continue cooking until the wine is reduced to half.

Add veal to mushrooms on medium heat. After 5 minutes remove veal to a hot platter.

Add the remaining wine to the pan. Add remaining butter. Bring to a boil, and then simmer for 4 minutes. Add parsley, and pour over the meat. Serve with steamed white rice.

PÂTÉ ∽

Serves 8

900g/2lb goose, duck or chicken
    livers

1 teaspoon salt

½ teaspoon freshly ground black
    pepper

Plain (all-purpose) flour, for sprinkling

175g/6oz/¾ cup (1½ sticks) soft butter

225g/8oz minced veal

2 medium onions, diced

¼ teaspoon ground cinnamon

¼ teaspoon freshly grated nutmeg

120ml/4fl oz/½ cup Rémy Martin
    cognac

250ml/8fl oz/1 cup chicken stock

Preheat oven to 180°C/350°F/Gas Mark 4.
Liberally butter a 23 x 7.5cm/9 x 3in loaf
tin.

Clean livers of all veins, gristle and fat.
Season with salt and pepper and dust with
flour.

In large sauté pan, melt 50g/2oz/¼ cup (½
stick) butter, and place veal and livers in
pan. Sauté on medium heat until done.
(When no blood comes from the veal and
livers, they are done.) Cool, and remove
from pan to warm plate.

Put remaining butter into pan. Melt, and
add onions. Sauté on medium heat until
translucent. Let cool.

Purée livers, veal and onions. Mix in
cinnamon, nutmeg and cognac, then
chicken stock.

Pour mixture into prepared loaf tin. Bake
30 minutes. Remove and cool. Place in
refrigerator with another loaf tin holding
two 425g/15oz cans vegetables on top of
pâté for 24 hours (to remove any air
pockets in the baked mixture). Slice and
serve cold.

MOULDED EGGS POLIGNAC

Serves 6

9 teaspoons butter, plus more for
   toast and garnish
6 truffle slices
6 large eggs
6 buttered toast rounds
2 teaspoons finely chopped fresh
   parsley

Preheat oven to 180°C/350°F/Gas Mark 4.

Melt 1½ teaspoons butter in each of six small moulds or ramekins. Lay a slice of truffle in the bottom of each mould. Break an egg into each mould, and set the moulds in a tin of hot water. Bake for 8 to 10 minutes, or until the whites are set and the yolks a little soft.

Remove the moulds from the hot water and let the eggs and truffles cool for a few minutes. Un-mould each egg and truffle onto a small round of buttered toast, and garnish with melted butter and parsley.

ENGLISH, PLEASE

T he London drawing room glowed beneath subdued
lighting. Antique furniture showed its age gracefully, and
our hostess, Sonia Orwell, was what she wanted to be: a
picture of an upper-class hoyden.

I was introduced to the guests and told that they were great
artists. One painter was the grandson of a famous psychiatrist,
another painter had the same name as a renowned eighteenth-
century English writer, and yet another was a trendy painter-
photographer. Sonia shook her mane of blond hair and told them
that I was writing a book.

The men gathered around me and asked pointed questions that
seemed at odds in such amiable quarters.

"What on earth do you find in London that you don't have in
the States?"

"Why do you come to England to write?"

"You can't escape racism, you know. English say all wogs begin
at Calley."

True, I didn't know from his accent that his Calley meant the
French town Calais, nor at that time did I know that the word wog
meant "nigger," but I knew they were being hostile to me, so I
responded in kind.

"I wanted to be in familiar surroundings. And you've just
shown me there are as many ignoramuses here as there are in the
United States. I didn't come here looking for anything. I brought

everything I need with me. I know it is more blessed to give than to receive, so I'm willing to donate some of my wit to those who need it so badly."

Sonia shook her hair and said, "You've found a match!" The men laughed at my retorts.

We had become fairly friendly by the time we were asked to come downstairs to dinner.

We sat at a beautiful table festooned with personal nosegays at each plate.

The first course was an onion tart. I had never tasted anything better. I chewed slowly, registering each flavor. The shortness of the crust backed up the sweetness of caramelized onions. Voices intruded into my reverie.

"Maya, yes, Maya, what do you think of contemporary composers?"

"Yes. Like John Cage?"

I said, "Well, for me the emperor has no clothes. I think he is an impostor."

Each artist, and even Sonia, began to shout at me. "You can't call John Cage an impostor."

I remembered fifteen years earlier being an impoverished dancer. I saved every penny of my money so that I could attend a John Cage concert. I sat happily in the cheapest seat waiting for the artist so many people held as one of the important figures of twentieth-century art.

John Cage and a stagehand appeared carrying a record player. They plugged it into a socket and left the stage.

As the audience waited, there was a click and after a few seconds there was another click. Then another click. And another click.

I looked at the program and it read something like "Traffic Light at the Corner of Sixty-fifth and Park Avenue."

I left the theater hurriedly, pushing myself past people who were rapt in ecstasy over the sound of a traffic light clicking.

On the street, I was spitting mad. I had given up too many slices of pizza and ice-cream cones and subway rides to be so insulted.

I repeated at Sonia's table, "Yes, I think he is a charlatan and a poseur."

The company looked at me with disgust.

"Obviously conversation with you will be impossible."

"Anyone ignorant enough to call Cage a poseur is too ignorant for social exchange."

"Where did you find her, Sonia?"

Sonia came out of the kitchen carrying a tray that held a beautiful roast pork and baked apples. I stood up.

"Thank you, Sonia. I realize I have to be in Bangkok in half an hour."

She followed me upstairs and to her front door.

"Maya, they really like you. They think of you as an equal or they wouldn't have talked that way."

"I will never be their equal and they will never be mine."

I walked down her front stairs and into the London night.

I could have kicked myself for having wasted an evening. Then I thought I didn't really waste the evening. I did meet up with a great onion tart, and I had had the time to linger over it. And (I hoped) I could solve its mystery.

ONION TART ∽

Serves 6

6–8 medium onions, thinly sliced

40g/1½oz/3 tablespoons butter or
   bacon fat

475ml/16fl oz/2 cups double (heavy)
   cream

3 large eggs, slightly beaten

1½ teaspoons salt

¼ teaspoon paprika

¼ teaspoon freshly ground black
   pepper

⅛ teaspoon freshly grated nutmeg

One 23cm/9in ready-baked shortcrust
   pastry case

Preheat oven to 230°C/450°F/Gas Mark 8 for 10 minutes.

Sauté onions in butter or bacon fat slowly until soft and golden.

Cool to room temperature. Add cream, eggs, salt, paprika, pepper and nutmeg to onions, mix well, and turn into pastry case.

Bake for 10 minutes. Then reduce oven temperature to 180°C/350°F/Gas Mark 4, and bake for 30 minutes longer, or until knife blade inserted in the tart comes out clean.

SWEET SOUTHERN MEMORIES

In the mid-1960s, Los Angeles was friendly but unfocused for me. Thanks to Frances Williams, whom I had known years earlier, I had a place to stay but no job, and my money was slipping away.

I had sounded like a dunce at the employment agency.

The young, serious social worker asked, "What was your last job?"

"I sang calypso and blues in a supper club."

She made notes and then asked, "Where was that?"

"In Oahu, Hawaii, Waikiki."

Her eyes opened. "Why did you stop?"

"I realized I don't sing very well."

She caught a breath. "Ahem, okay. What did you do before that?"

"I was an administrative assistant at a university."

"Oh." For a moment she found relief. "So, you can type?"

"No, but I can file."

The relief vanished. "At what university did you work?"

"At the University of Ghana in West Africa."

The interviewer let the pencil fall from her fingers. "I don't have anything for you. You may be unemployable."

As was to be expected, Frances Williams knew someone who could offer me a job. She asked if I could cook.

I said, "I cook very well."

She asked, "Southern?"

I said, "Of course, but I don't really want a job as a cook."

She said, "No, that's not the job I'm looking at for you. Let me tell you about Phil, who handles random research systems for large companies like Kellogg's and General Foods and Ivory Soap."

She said Phil had a publicity agency and was a good ole white boy from the South. He was so homesick that he would break down and cry if you mentioned fried chicken.

She said she would invite him to her house, and if I made a southern brunch, she was pretty certain he would give me a job. She asked, "Are you sure you can cook? I can't help you because that would be lying and lying won't help anybody in the end, and I tell the truth. Tell a lie and you'll never be finished scheming." That was Frances Williams's motto.

She offered to buy the brunch ingredients and said she'd call Phil and a few other friends so he wouldn't feel set up.

I said, "But we are setting him up."

"Not at all," she said, "unless you want to think I'm setting you up. Here's how I see it. My friends and I are going to find out if you can really cook. If so, and you cook southern, Phil is going to think he's waking up in a dream and you'll get a job. Friends of mine who haven't seen me or each other in months will have a great time."

I made a list for her. She asked, "No grits? You'll have a southern breakfast without grits?"

I said, "They won't be missed."

On Sunday morning, I went early to Frances's kitchen, and when everyone arrived I was sitting calmly in the living room, which was alive with the aromas of sage and caramelized brown sugar.

Frances introduced me to Phil. "She's just come from Africa." His face was a mask of disinterest. "But she's from the South." A little interest awakened his features.

"From where?"

I said, "A little hamlet in Arkansas, twenty-five miles from Texarkana."

He gave me a smile grudgingly. "You miss it, don't you?"

Frances spoke before I had to lie. "She's out here looking for a job, and she's so sweet she came over here and made our brunch. The whole thing."

I had his full attention. "What did you cook?"

I said, "Sausage and eggs."

He asked in a little boy's voice, "And grits?"

I said, "No," and the smile slid down to the floor. I quickly added, "I made spoon bread."

"Spoon bread. You said spoon bread? I haven't had spoon bread since I left Birmingham."

Seeing him so pleased delighted me. I added, "I make my own sausage, and we'll also have fried apples and homemade biscuits." His smile was so winning I could have hugged him.

Brunch was offered buffet-style. After Phil served himself, he sat alone on a window seat. I watched as his eyes visited each item on his plate. Only after he assured himself that he had seen what he thought he had seen did he begin to eat. He would put a forkful of food in his mouth and then he would seem to disappear. He slowly chewed his way back to his Alabama childhood.

Later I saw Frances and him talking out on the patio. When they came in, he headed straight to me.

"You can start on Monday. It doesn't pay much, but it's easy work. Fran says you are a writer. I just want you to give me your recipe for spoon bread and for biscuits and for sausage. Oh yeah, and for fried apples, too. Well, if you can write half as good as you can cook, you are going to be famous."

SPOON BREAD ∞

Serves 6 to 8

225g/8oz/2 cups white cornmeal

115g/4oz/1 cup plain (all-purpose) flour

4 teaspoons baking powder

2 teaspoons salt

350ml/12fl oz/1½ cups cold water

250ml/8fl oz/1 cup boiling water

25g/1oz/2 tablespoons (¼ stick) butter, melted

2 large eggs, beaten

350ml/12fl oz/1½ cups milk

Preheat oven to 190°C/375°F/Gas Mark 5. Butter a 2 litre/3½ pint/8 cup (2 quart) ovenproof casserole dish.

Sift together cornmeal, flour, baking powder and salt. Stir in cold water. Add boiling water, and stir vigorously. Add remaining ingredients, and mix well. Pour into casserole dish. Bake for 1 hour, or until firm and browned. Serve at once.

FRIED APPLES ∞

Serves 6

6 Granny Smith apples

2 McIntosh apples or 2 red-skinned eating apples

50g/2oz/¼ cup (½ stick) butter

2 tablespoons brown sugar

250ml/8fl oz/1 cup water

½ teaspoon ground cinnamon

¼ teaspoon freshly grated nutmeg

Quarter and core apples, but do not peel. Melt butter in large frying pan, and place apples skin-side down in pan. Sprinkle with brown sugar, and add water. Add cinnamon and nutmeg, cover, and cook very slowly over low heat until tender and candied. Eat hot.

HOMEMADE BISCUITS ⌒

Makes about 1 dozen biscuits

350g/12oz/3 cups plain (all-purpose)
    flour

5 teaspoons baking powder

½ teaspoon salt

75g/3oz/½ cup shortening, white
    cooking fat or lard

250ml/8fl oz/1 cup milk

Plain (all-purpose) flour, for sprinkling

Preheat oven to 180°C/350°F/Gas Mark 4.

Sift flour, baking powder and salt together in a mixing bowl. Cut in or rub in shortening until mixture resembles coarse cornmeal. Add milk using more if needed, to make a soft dough.

Roll out dough on floured board to 2cm/¾in thickness. Cut into 5cm/2in rounds. (If biscuit cutter is not at hand, use water glass dipped in flour.) Bake on well-greased baking sheet for 25 minutes (longer if you want them browner).

SAUSAGE ∞

Serves 6

900g/2lb lean boneless pork

115g/4oz pork fat

2 teaspoons salt

1 teaspoon dried sage

1 teaspoon dried red pepper or chilli
  flakes

1 teaspoon freshly ground black
  pepper

Mince pork with pork fat. Combine salt, sage, red pepper flakes, pepper and minced meat. Using 2 heaped tablespoons of meat mixture each, roll into balls, then flatten. Fry in medium-hot skillet until no blood is visible.

FOWL COMMUNICATION

J essica Mitford, who was called Decca, was a Briton transplanted among the hoi polloi in Oakland, California. To be more precise, Decca Mitford was an English aristocrat who once chose to become a card-carrying member of the Communist Party and live in a working-class town in northern California.

She and her lawyer husband, Robert Treuhaft, later left the party because they concluded that the organization was reneging on some of the high and lofty political and ethical ideals that had first appealed to them.

Bob and Decca lived in a commodious, rambling 1920s California bungalow, where they entertained celebrities and others, from the legendary blues singer Leadbelly to the odd felon on the run.

Bob was always the cook, specializing in the very best Boston baked beans, duck pâté, and butterflied roast leg of lamb. Decca mostly tidied up.

Decca and Bob's group was planning a large gala, and as preparatory chores were appointed most people thought Decca couldn't be much help in the kitchen, so she was asked to order the chickens, which more experienced members would then cook.

Decca telephoned the number she had been given for the chickens.

"I'd like to order fifty frying chickens to be delivered to a social hall on Wednesday at ten o'clock a.m."

"Do you want them dressed or undressed?"

She said, "Undressed of course."

Decca told me, "You must know that banqueting is also a part of the struggle."

She went to the meeting hall on Wednesday and was utterly shocked to see fifty chickens delivered with feathers, heads, necks, and feet attached.

She shouted at the deliverymen, "Why do they have all these things on them? I told you I wanted them undressed."

She was informed that in poultry parlance undressed meant with all the things on them and in them.

Decca called headquarters and told her story. She asked if there were any communists who knew how to dress a chicken.

Within an hour, chicken pluckers and cleaners were at the hall. They immediately began defeathering and disemboweling the chickens. When Decca saw the amount of work that was necessary, she was stricken with gratitude. No one had ever seen her so apologetic.

"Listen, I'm very sorry. And all of this brought about by my saying undressed rather than dressed."

One of the pluckers said, "You couldn't have known, Decca. You speak English. We speak American. We also speak poultry. What you do, you do so well. You deserve to take one of these chickens home fully dressed."

She accepted the chicken. She brought it home and opened a bottle of white wine, and quickly drank one half. Without benefit of recipe, she began to cook. She put the chicken into a casserole pot along with celery, onions, seasoning, and the rest of the wine.

She called her husband and told him what she had done, and she went to bed. When Bob came home, he removed the pot and opened it. The chicken was beautifully cooked.

From that time, I have cooked that dish following Decca's recipe and served it once a month, both to my delight and to the pleasure of my guests.

It is still called Decca's Chicken, Drunkard Style.

DECCA'S CHICKEN, DRUNKARD STYLE ∽

Serves 6

1 chicken (about 1.3kg/3lb), cut into
  pieces
1 stick celery, chopped
1 medium onion, chopped
1 carrot, peeled and chopped
2 cloves garlic, minced
120ml/4fl oz/½ cup water
2 teaspoons salt
½ bottle Chardonnay
Freshly ground black pepper, to taste

First, drink 1 glass of wine.

Preheat oven to 190°C/375°F/Gas Mark 5.

Wash chicken. Put all ingredients into a large, heavy ovenproof casserole dish, and place in oven. Bake for 2 hours. Serve hot.

If you want thick gravy, remove chicken and vegetables from casserole. Add 3 tablespoons cornflour (cornstarch) and 175ml/6fl oz/¾ cup water to hot broth. Put back into oven until thickened to desired consistency.

BOB'S BOSTON BAKED BEANS ∽

Serves 6

350g/12oz/2 cups dried Great
   Northern beans or dried haricot
   beans

115g/4oz lean salt pork

1 medium onion, diced

1 teaspoon salt

185g/6½oz/½ cup light molasses

½ teaspoon dried mustard

1 tablespoon granulated sugar

Pick over beans, discarding stones or debris. Rinse beans, then soak overnight in enough water to cover.

Next morning, drain beans. Fill large saucepan with water, and add beans, pork, onion and salt. Boil, covered, until semi-tender, about 45 to 50 minutes. Watch carefully – water must be kept above beans in pan.

Preheat oven to 150°C/300°F/Gas Mark 2.

Mix remaining ingredients with beans. Pour into an ovenproof casserole dish. Bury pork in beans, leaving rind exposed. Cover. Bake for 4 hours.

M.F.K. FISHER AND A WHITE BEAN FEAST

Sonoma, California, was a working town. Some camera-wielding tourists did visit on weekends, lured by the romance of the ancient Spanish missions and proximity of the local vineyards, but the town was so busy serving itself there was no time for it to become quaint, precious, or twee.

Cattle ranchers, vineyard workers, farmers, and shop owners used the streets and the parks as if they were extensions of their own homes. Teachers, professors, members of the religious community, and artists held proprietary feelings about the town. Aging hippies mixed with young malcontents; singers from the local chorale walked shoulder to shoulder with the rich local barons. During the golden seventies we moved from Berkeley to Sonoma. My husband and I had come to know the area by visiting our friends David Bouverie and M. F. K. Fisher, who lived there.

The town liked itself so much that it gave itself a party once a year. The summer fête was called the Ox-Roast. During the roast weekend, locals would crowd the town square, bringing their own victuals. (I don't remember seeing anyone actually eating the ox that was cooked on a spit, which took ten strong men to turn.)

We moved to Sonoma during that annual celebration, and I phoned Mary Frances to learn if she planned to visit the public picnic. She told me she would not be coming that year.

Then I asked her to dinner in our new place. When I added that my husband would come and pick her up, she said she would be happy to come.

There was a chic cookery shop on the town square. The two men who owned the store, Gene and Dick, matched it perfectly.

They had an eastern vogue about them. They welcomed me warmly when I entered the shop. They'd heard that I was moving to Sonoma and they were happy to help me.

They supposed my pots and pans were still in boxes, and they had made a list of the best restaurants in town, which they were sure I would need. Most of my cookware was indeed still packed away, but I explained that I had invited someone for dinner that evening and that I would need to buy a few pots to use that night.

"You are cooking in pots you have not tried? Maybe your guests are not too keen on cuisine and they will never know."

I said, "My guest is very keen on cuisine. Her name is M. F. K. Fisher."

"You mean … you don't mean … Mary Frances Kennedy Fisher?"

I said, "Yes."

Dick looked at me as if I were Julia Child and had just flown in the door with saucepans for wings.

"You are going to cook for M. F. K. Fisher?"

I said, "She has to eat also."

"We've asked her to have dinner, but we've taken her to restaurants. We would never cook for her."

Gene asked, "What do you plan to cook?"

I said, "A cassoulet."

They both laughed out loud. I defended my choice. "I know that fall is a great season for cassoulet, but after all it is a peasant dish – so any season is great if you like beans and meat."

"Please let us know how Mary Frances enjoyed your dinner." They wore wry smiles as we said good-bye.

I began preparing the cassoulet, and my husband opened enough boxes for me to set a good table.

When he brought Mary Frances back, we had a trio of good stories, laughter, and good wine.

Mary Frances was easy with the chaos of my new house.

She said, "All new houses are the same. They search around a few months for their true personalities. This is an amiable space. I think you'll both be very happy here." We had an aperitif then went to the table.

I told her that the owners of the cookery shop were shocked that I would cook for her.

She reminded me of what had happened to her in Hollywood. She said that in the 1930s and 1940s she had written scripts in Hollywood but her prowess as a cook had preceded her. The glamorous stars had invited her to their Beverly Hills and Bel Air mansions for drinks and canapés, cocktails and hors d'oeuvres. She said she could smell dinner as it was being cooked, but hosts were so intimidated by her reputation that after drinks they would have their chauffeurs take her back to the hotel.

She said she would have given anything for a home-cooked hamburger or a decent omelet made in the kitchen of a friend.

I served the cassoulet with good Sonoma bread.

She spent a few quiet seconds savoring each flavor, but she was such an adept social guest that the conversation never lagged nor did the food get cold.

We took dessert, a simple flan, out by the swimming pool. She was the perfect guest. She left at the proper time, not too early, nor too late.

My husband took her home. When he returned, he said, "She really enjoyed the evening." I wasn't all that sure. I thought the beans had been a little mushy.

One week later I received a thank-you note with a few comments on the state of the world. After her signature, there was a P.S.:

"Dear Maya, thank you. That was the first honest cassoulet I have eaten in years."

CASSOULET ∽

Serves 8 to 10

700g/1lb 9oz/4 cups pea beans,
   washed and drained
2 litres/3½ pints/8 cups (2 quarts)
   water
1 tablespoon salt
2 cloves garlic, mashed
2 carrots, peeled and quartered
2 medium onions, left whole
Bouquet garni made of fresh parsley,
   4 cloves, bay leaf and fresh thyme
   (see p. 9)
75g/3oz/½ cup salt pork, diced
2 tablespoons duck or goose
   drippings or olive oil
675g/1½lb lean boneless pork, cubed
450g/1lb boneless lamb, cubed
2 small Bermuda or standard onions,
   chopped
75g/3oz/1 cup chopped spring
   (green) onions (white and green
   parts)
115g/4oz/1 cup thinly sliced celery
250ml/8fl oz/1 cup passata or tomato
   juice
250ml/8fl oz/1 cup dry white wine
1 garlic sausage or Polish sausage,
   sliced into 5mm/¼in pieces
1 roasted duck or roasted goose,
   removed from bones and cut into
   bite-size pieces
1 roasted chicken, removed from
   bones and cut into bite-size
   pieces

Combine beans, water and salt in large saucepan. Let stand overnight, or boil for 2 minutes and let soak for 1 hour.

Add garlic, carrots, onions, bouquet garni and salt pork, and bring to a boil. Simmer, covered, for 1 hour, skimming surface as needed.

Heat drippings in large skillet. Add pork and lamb, and brown on all sides over medium heat. Add to bean mixture.

In same skillet, sauté all onions and the celery until soft. Add passata and wine, and simmer for 5 minutes. Add to beans together with sausage. Simmer covered over low heat for 1 hour, or until beans and meats are tender. If necessary, add a little water to prevent scorching. Skim off excess fat. Discard bouquet garni.

Preheat oven to 180°C/350°F/Gas Mark 4.

Transfer mixture to large ovenproof casserole dish, and add pieces of duck and chicken. Bake covered for 30 minutes, stirring a couple times. Check occasionally for moisture; if necessary, add a little wine or water. Adjust seasoning. Serve hot.

FROM PIZZA TO
CLAIBORNE AND BACK

The host said we were eating braised beef and potatoes. We knew she had an inordinate amount of false modesty and that in fact she had served us an exquisite *daube de boeuf* with potatoes Annette. Her dessert almost knocked us back from the dining table. Like fried ice cream, it was oxymoronic. She ended her splendid dinner by serving a cold lemon mousse with a baked meringue topping. We were floored.

We were an eclectic assemblage who had developed, without planning, a habit of cooking for each other once a month. At the end of each incredible meal (each host tried to outdo the last), the next cook would volunteer.

Everyone knew that I should be the next host, but I hesitated. How does one follow Auguste Escoffier or M. F. K. Fisher? I rolled my trepidation into a pill and swallowed it. "Come to me next month, I'll be ready."

My friends looked at me pityingly.

Once swallowed, the fear remained buried, and I tamped it further down with the knowledge that after all I was a good cook and I was in New York City where anything I thought I needed could be found. I toyed with duck galantine and sautéed veal with sherry and macadamia nuts. I considered a ten-boy lamb curry, placing ten relishes in my mind's eye: grated coconut, golden raisins, Major Grey's mango chutney, diced avocado, diced onion, tomatoes, fried onions, banana, cucumbers vinaigrette, and plain yogurt. Although no award of any kind was at stake, the competitive spirit among the circle of cooking friends was alive and kicking. I did not dare risk those dishes I'd thought of against the dinner we had just finished.

When the group came to my house, I fell back on my Arkansas upbringing. I gave them a black-eyed pea soup and southern fried chicken with homemade biscuits. For dessert I offered New Orleans pecan pie with a bourbon sauce. The food was a knockout, I had held on to my reputation as a peer among peers.

Bebe was a single parent who bragged in her heavy Uruguayan accent that she couldn't cook and wouldn't cook. She said she was raising her tall strapping teenage son, Bo, on dry cereal and milk in the morning, pizza and a salad for lunch, and the same thing for dinner. Her presence in our circle of writers who considered themselves to be gourmet cooks was inexplicable, but she did belong. She was a businesswoman and a writer who was very funny and interesting.

As we were having dessert, Bebe shocked us by saying, "Come to my apartment for dinner next month." We almost choked on our pecan pie.

"No, no. We know you don't know how to ..."

"Really, I had planned to be in Bangkok that ..."

"Oh, no, you shouldn't have to do this."

"Okay. We'll come and eat pizza and salad."

"I like a good pizza. A good pizza is a work of art ..."

Bebe said, "No, we won't eat pizza. I will cook."

When the evening was over, everybody left laughing in their hands. Would we really be given take-out pizza for dinner and would she at least make the salad dressing at home?

Four weeks later, we met in the lobby of her building, still snickering.

"What do you think?"

"I brought my Tums."

"I brought Alka-Seltzer for everybody."

When we emerged from the elevator on her floor, the hall was redolent of mouthwatering aromas.

"At least somebody on her floor knows how to cook."

"Or maybe just someone in the building."

We laughed as Bebe opened the door, but our laughter ended when we entered her apartment. As we followed her to the living room, we knew that the aromas emanated from her kitchen. We were stunned. Her son, Bo, brought out a tray of drinks with a filled ice bucket, tongs, olives, and slices of lemon. We were invited to make our own drinks as Bebe disappeared into the kitchen. We could find nothing to say, so we offered blank faces to each other as we helped ourselves to libation. Bo emerged from the kitchen again, with a larger tray, which held oversized cups. He said, "Gazpacho, please take one." The Spanish tomato soup was as cold as it should have been and rich with bite sizes of cucumber and finely chopped onion.

Many would-be cooks attempt to make gazpacho but conclude with horrific nonedible, nonpotable results. This one was as perfect a blend as any I had ever tasted. Bebe stayed in the kitchen as we chewed the crunchy vegetables and drank the beautifully flavored cold tomato soup.

Bo collected the empty cups and asked if we would sit to table. There were place cards. We knew Bebe hadn't been brought up in a barn, but nothing about her prepared us for this sophistication. After we were seated, she stepped into the dining room and announced, "Dinner is served." When she turned back into the kitchen, the smile on her face was sweet enough to rot teeth. She and Bo returned, placing on the table *petit pois* with pearl onions in a cream sauce, haricots verts in vinaigrette, and twice-baked potatoes and mushroom gravy. The pièce de résistance was a beef Wellington.

We stood and applauded and she joined in the admiring laughter. Each of us knew the complexity of building a beef

Wellington. How the duxelles must be prepared while the loin is in the oven. How the loin must be cooling as the short pastry rests in the refrigerator. How the pâté must be at a spreadable consistency before the duxelles is patted in place. Bebe said she would love to tell us when we finished eating how a noncook had managed to bring off a four-star dinner.

We sat with small bowls of good commercial ice cream for dessert and she described her day. At 10 a.m., she telephoned *The New York Times* and asked to speak to food editor Craig Claiborne. She would not be pacified by his assistant. When Mr. Claiborne answered, Bebe accented her already heavy accent and, with her flair for dramatics, began to cry. "Mr. Claiborne, I am the wife of the Uruguay ambassador and I have invited eight couples of diplomats and two foreign vice presidents with their wives for dinner. This morning" – here a loud outburst of sobs – "my cook and his staff walked out in a huff. Oh my, Mr. Claiborne, I fear an international incident. I had the cook send out the menu, and I cannot possibly deliver." According to Bebe, Craig Claiborne asked what the menu was.

She replied, "Gazpacho, beef Wellington, *petit pois*, twice-baked potatoes, and haricots verts."

She told him she had all the ingredients and a grown daughter who could help her. He assured her that he would keep the telephone open all day and would walk her through each dish. All she had to do was follow his instructions to the letter.

According to her, he did keep the telephone open, and from the success of the dinner, she certainly followed his instructions.

As we left her apartment, she said, "I did this to prove to you unbearable egotists that cooking is no big thing. After we eat up all the leftovers, Bo and I will be back to pizza and salad. I'm not a cook and look what I was able to do."

I think Bebe is a great cook. No one knew it then.

I believe one can be born a great cook, achieve the status of a great cook, or have the greatness of cooking thrust upon her.

Bebe is probably head chef at New York's Four Seasons today.

Wherever she is, here are my recipes for beef Wellington, gazpacho, *petit pois*, twice-baked potatoes, and haricots verts.

BEEF WELLINGTON ∞

Serves 6 to 8

900g–1.3kg/2–3lb lean beef fillet
 (tenderloin)

Salt and freshly ground black pepper,
 to taste

1 small onion, minced

2 sticks celery, minced

2 portobello mushrooms, minced

25g/1oz/2 tablespoons (¼ stick)
 butter

1 sheet Puffed Pastry (recipe follows)

225g/8oz chicken liver pâté

1 large egg

120ml/4fl oz/½ cup water

Preheat oven to 190°C/375°F/Gas Mark 5.

Season beef with salt and pepper, and roast for 45 minutes. Interior beef temperature should be 57°C–63°C/135°F–145°F for medium. Remove from oven. Let cool. Reduce oven temperature to 160°C/325°F/Gas Mark 3.

In large skillet, sauté onion, celery, mushrooms and butter – this is called duxelles.

Take Puffed Pastry from refrigerator, and roll out on floured board. If pastry is too dry, add cold water sparingly. Sheet should measure 7.5cm/3in longer and 13cm/5in wider than joint. Place half the duxelles on pastry. Place joint on the duxelles mixture. Cover joint with pâté. Put the remaining duxelles on tops and sides of the joint. Bring pastry dough up to cover sides, ends, and top of the joint.

Mix egg and water together. With pastry brush, brush egg wash on sides, ends, and top of pastry. Bake for 40 minutes.

PUFFED PASTRY ∽

225g/8oz/2 cups sifted plain (all-
   purpose) flour
½ teaspoon baking powder
½ teaspoon salt
115g/4oz/⅔ cup soft shortening or
   white vegetable fat
1 large egg, beaten with 2
   tablespoons milk

Sift together flour, baking powder and salt in mixing bowl. Cut in or rub in shortening. Mix in egg mixture lightly. Chill for 1 hour.

GAZPACHO ∽

Serves 6 to 8

½ clove garlic, minced
1 teaspoon salt
3 tablespoons olive oil
3 tablespoons vinegar
600ml/1 pint/2½ cups cold water
4 tomatoes, diced
475ml/16fl oz/2 cups tomato juice,
   chilled
1 green (bell) pepper, seeded and
   diced
2 tablespoons minced onion
1 cucumber, diced
2 sticks celery, diced
40g/1½oz/½ cup bread croutons

Blend garlic, salt, oil, vinegar and water together. Add tomatoes and tomato juice. Serve green pepper, onion, cucumber, celery and croutons on the side. Each person can choose veggies and croutons as desired.

PETIT POIS ∽

Serves 4 to 6

450g/1lb/4 cups fresh small green
   peas (shelled weight)
475ml/16fl oz/2 cups chicken stock
   or water
225g/8oz cooked baby (pearl) onions
Salt and freshly ground black pepper,
   to taste
25g/1oz/2 tablespoons (¼ stick)
   butter
2 tablespoons plain (all-purpose) flour
250ml/8fl oz/1 cup cold milk

In small, heavy-based saucepan, cook peas in stock over medium heat for 5 minutes. Add onions and cook another 5 minutes. Drain.

Season peas and onions with salt and pepper and butter. Mix flour with milk, then add to peas and onions, stirring quickly. Cook over medium heat, stirring constantly for 10 minutes. If cream sauce is too thick, add water to desired thinness.

TWICE-BAKED POTATOES

Serves 4

4 large baking potatoes

1 teaspoon vegetable oil

4 spring (green) onions (white and
green parts), minced

250ml/8fl oz/1 cup soured (sour)
cream

25g/1oz/2 tablespoons (¼ stick)
butter

Salt and freshly ground black pepper,
to taste

50g/2oz/½ cup grated cheddar
cheese

Preheat oven to 180°C/350°F/Gas Mark 4.

Scrub and pat dry potatoes, and grease
with oil. Bake for 45 minutes. Remove
from oven, and increase oven temperature
to 190°C/375°F/Gas Mark 5.

When potatoes have cooled, cut
lengthwise, and scrape centre from
potatoes carefully, leaving 3mm/⅛in so that
walls of potatoes will not collapse. Mix
remaining ingredients in bowl, and mash
with potato flesh. Divide mashed potato
mixture equally among potato shells. Bake
for 30 minutes.

HARICOTS VERTS ∽

Serves 6

900g/2lb thin green beans

½ teaspoon salt

3 litres/5¼ pints/12 cups (3 quarts)
   water

Vinaigrette (recipe follows)

Cook beans over medium heat in pan of salted water until crispy tender. Drain well, cool, and pour Vinaigrette over beans.

VINAIGRETTE ∽

Makes about 350ml/12fl oz/1½ cups

120ml/4fl oz/½ cup water

250ml/8fl oz/1 cup cider vinegar

½ teaspoon dried tarragon

½ teaspoon dried thyme

3 tablespoons olive oil

1 clove garlic, minced

Salt, to taste

Bring water to boil in saucepan. Add vinegar to water and scald for 5 minutes. Remove from heat, and cool. Add dried herbs, olive oil and garlic, and season with salt.

SISTERLY TRANSLATION

Rosa Guy and I became good friends in New York City during the late 1950s. She was Trinidadian-born and brought to the United States when she was seven years old. I had been born in Missouri and raised everywhere. Still, we had much in common. We were nearly the same age, enjoyed music, food, dancing, and relished the company of high-spirited men. We were both good cooks and admired each other's skills. She was a founding member of the Harlem Writers Guild, and because I also belonged to the association some other members tried to set up a cooking competition between us. We refused to be drawn into such an unproductive use of energy.

Rosa told me that Trinidadians make and eat souse during the Christmas and New Year's holidays. I told her that people in Stamps, Arkansas, where I grew up, do the same. She always invited friends to celebrate Thanksgiving at her house but now suggested that we might like to do New Year's at my apartment. She and I would both make souse to help celebrate. We would eat and then go to Central Park to drink champagne and watch fireworks.

New Year's Eve bloomed and Rosa arrived early with her souse. I confess to being a little nervous. My grandmother was the best cook I had ever known and I had used her recipe. Rosa set her bowl down on the kitchen table and lifted the top. I must have given a little scream.

She asked, "What's the matter?"

I said, "Those are pig's feet."

She said, "Yes, of course. It's souse."

I pulled my souse from the refrigerator and ran a knife around the side of the dish and unmolded the contents.

She asked, "What is that?"

I said, "Souse."

We looked at each other, then at our so different dishes. There was nothing for it but to laugh.

She asked, "You call that souse?"

"Everybody I know in Arkansas calls that souse and we call what you've got pickled pig's feet."

She said, "Of course you make souse out of pig's feet. Here, have a taste."

Her dish was wonderful. The skin on the pig's feet was white and there were rings of onion and wedges of crisp green peppers. I ate the piece she pulled off and it was exactly what we called pickled pig's feet.

I said, "Taste this." Then I took a slice from my loaf-molded souse.

She ate it. "That's good. That's hog head cheese."

I said, "Yes, but we also call it souse."

When the guests arrived, we served them hog head cheese and pig's feet and unending champagne.

When a person relished my dish, I would look over to Rosa and smirk. Each time her souse received a compliment, she would all but stick out her tongue at me. I imagined had we been alone and ten years old, she would have put both her hands behind her ears and moved them forward and I would have made a face and said, Nyah, nyah, nyah, nyah.

For many years we brought in the new year in Central Park with champagne after having eaten souse, hog head cheese, and pickled pig's feet in my apartment.

PICKLED PIG'S FEET, OR SOUSE

Serves 6

6 pig's feet

2 tablespoons salt

½ teaspoon freshly ground black
pepper

475ml/16fl oz/2 cups cider vinegar (or
more, to taste)

5 whole cloves

1 tablespoon granulated sugar

1 teaspoon dried red pepper or chilli
flakes

3 large green (bell) peppers, seeded
and quartered

3 large onions, sliced into rings

Scrape and clean pig's feet. Place in large saucepan, and add boiling water to cover. Cook over medium heat until pig's feet are tender, about 4 hours. Add 1 tablespoon salt, ¼ teaspoon black pepper, 250ml/8fl oz/1 cup vinegar, 3 cloves, ½ tablespoon sugar, and ½ teaspoon red pepper flakes to broth. Cook 1 more hour.

Remove pig's feet from hot broth and cool.

Make another brine with remaining salt, black pepper, vinegar, cloves, sugar and red pepper flakes. Boil 15 minutes, then cool. Pour over cooled pig's feet. Place in refrigerator. Add wedges of green pepper and rings of onion to cold brine. Serve cold.

HOG HEAD CHEESE ∽

Makes 6 to 8 bread-loaf tins

2.25kg/5lb pig's feet

450g/1lb pig's ears

900g/2lb pork joint

1½ bottles Chardonnay

475ml/16fl oz/2 cups cider vinegar

1 large onion, studded with 6 cloves

8 sticks celery

5 bay leaves

10 black peppercorns

5 x 25g/1oz packets powdered
   gelatine (Knox gelatin)

3 teaspoons salt

3 teaspoons freshly ground black
   pepper

2 red (bell) peppers

Gherkins (cornichons) (optional)

In large saucepan, place pig's feet, ears and pork joint in wine and vinegar, and add enough water to cover. Place clove-studded onion, celery, bay leaves and peppercorns in cheesecloth bag, and add to pan.

Mix gelatine in 475ml/16fl oz/2 cups cool water, and add to pan along with salt, pepper and red peppers. Bring to a boil, and simmer about 4 hours, skimming the surface as it cooks. Cool, then strain, reserving liquid. Carefully remove all bones.

Cut up pig's ears, meat from pig's feet, and pork joint. Place in large bowl, and mix well. Check seasoning and return strained liquid to mixture. Pour into 6 loaf tins, or more if needed. Cover with cling film or plastic wrap, and put into refrigerator for 5 or more hours. When cool and set, turn out of tins onto cutting board. Slice and serve like pâté. Place each slice on salad plate, and add a few gherkins, if desired.

DOLLY AND SHERRY AND MAKING SISTERS

Dolly Mcpherson and I met at a party in Rosa Guy's home. Before she left, she invited me to her house for brunch the next morning. She said the invitation included Rosa. I thanked her and said I would come but that I wasn't sure about Rosa. I knew that in Rosa's house, after a rough Saturday night, Sunday morning always came late and didn't come easily. To my surprise, Rosa said yes, she would love to come. She wanted to see what someone so proper would serve for brunch.

Dolly's apartment was ready to be photographed for *House Beautiful*. In the living room a Federal nineteenth-century sofa sat on a lilac wall-to-wall carpet. An antique sewing table functioned as a side table while Queen Anne chairs surrounded a Duncan Phyfe table. Her walls were filled with fine art. Dolly was graced in a long housecoat. We had laughed together so quickly the night before that I had not noticed her very formal manners.

She served us good sherry in beautiful crystal glasses. I complimented her on their beauty and she said she had picked them up in France during her tour as a Fulbright Scholar.

Had the aromas from the kitchen not burgeoned with savory promises, I would have thought that maybe she was too highfalutin to cook for my taste.

I told her the food smelled inviting, then asked if she had some scotch. She said yes, and when Rosa said she'd like scotch as well Dolly said she would join us but with a sherry.

On her last trip from the kitchen, she announced that brunch was served.

Her dining table could have groaned under the weight of her offerings. Parsleyed egg noodles shone under a lathering of butter, and in another dish string beans looked crisp and pert. There was a loaf of warm bread on a cutting board and a lovely platter of sautéed chicken livers and onions. A gravy boat filled with dark brown sauce sat nearby.

It looked good enough to eat. I hoped it was. The livers earned my lifelong respect. They were well done but still soft, and the gravy was delicious without the well-known bitterness so often found in liver gravy. The beans were tender but still had some crunchy character, and the crust of the bread was crisp while the soft inside was warm enough to make the room-temperature butter submit.

Rosa smiled at the table with approval.

When we finished brunch, Dolly said now she would have a scotch. She liked to have a full meal before she drank liquor. That sounded reasonable to me.

On the strength of the perfectly cooked brunch and on the chemistry that passed between us, I thought I'd like to have Dolly for my sister-friend.

That was nearly forty years ago and we now live in the same town and each of us has spent decades working at the same university. We still say hallelujah for our sisterhood and I am still praising Dolly's chicken livers and gravy. And I have become used to having a sherry before dinner, with the meal, and a scotch after.

CHICKEN LIVERS ∽

Serves 4

450g/1lb chicken livers

Salt and freshly ground black pepper,
   to taste

90g/3½oz/¾ cup plain (all-purpose)
   flour

3 tablespoons vegetable oil

2 tablespoons diced celery

2 tablespoons minced spring (green)
   onions (white and green parts)

1 medium onion, finely diced

475ml/16fl oz/2 cups chicken broth
   or chicken stock

75ml/2½fl oz/⅓ cup good-quality dry
   sherry

Wash and separate chicken livers, and pat dry. Season with salt and pepper and dredge in 50g/2oz/½ cup flour. Heat 2 tablespoons oil in large skillet, and sauté livers for 2 minutes on each side. Remove livers from skillet.

Add remaining oil to skillet, and sauté celery and all onions until translucent. Add remaining flour to skillet. When brown, add chicken broth. Cook for 3 minutes, stirring constantly. Put livers back in skillet, and add sherry. Cover, and cook for 5 minutes. Serve at once.

BUTTERED NOODLES ∽

Serves 4

½ teaspoon salt

2 litres/3½ pints/8 cups (2 quarts)
　water

450g/1lb packet egg noodles

25g/1oz/2 tablespoons (¼ stick)
　butter, softened

1 tablespoon finely chopped fresh
　parsley

In large saucepan, bring salted water to a boil. Add noodles. Cook over medium to high heat for 10 minutes, or until desired tenderness. Drain. Mix butter and parsley with noodles, and serve at once.

WRITER'S BLOCK

There were bricks in my mattress and rocks in my pillow and no rest at all in my bed. On the same lumpy surface my husband lay snoring gently, a look of sweet satisfaction on his face. I so envied his delicious peace that I was tempted to pinch the skin on his inner arm, but he deserved better treatment than that so I decided to get up and leave the bed and the indulgence of slumber to him. Stealthily I began to slide out of the bed. When my feet touched the floor, I pressed both hands on the mattress. I didn't want him to realize that I was getting up so I continued to press on the mattress releasing tension slowly until I could stand up straight and my husband could sleep on undisturbed.

I went into the kitchen and poured a glass of good Chardonnay. I had to confront the stress which kept me from my rest. The truth was my writing was going badly. Or to put it directly, my writing was not going at all.

A sample of my work made me cry:

A RAT

SAT

ON A MAT

THAT'S THAT.

I was working on a fourth book, and although the others had been well received, it seemed to me this one would reveal to the world that I was a charlatan and couldn't write my way out of a brown paper sack.

I decided to cook a complicated dish, which would take my mind off the exacting task of writing. I chose to make chocolate éclairs with whipped cream and custard filling.

From the moment I decided to cook, I forgot about writing. Gone was my concern with nouns, pronouns, verbs, and dangling participles. I had made cream puffs and profiteroles before but never éclairs, so I had to concentrate.

I finished the dough and measured it for twelve éclairs. I decided to make six with custard filling and the rest filled with whipped cream. I turned on both ovens and put three éclairs on each cookie sheet and placed them on the middle rack of each oven. I made the custard and started the whipped cream.

I put a large block of unsweetened chocolate in the top of a double boiler and turned the fire low so the chocolate could melt.

When the oven whistle let me know that the pastries were done, I opened the oven door and nearly fainted. I had measured dough the size of six large cigars, three on each cookie sheet. They had grown into loaves the size of giant Italian bread. I took them out and put the next load into the oven and was handed back six more giant loaves.

While they cooled, I made more custard and more whipped cream and warmed more unsweetened chocolate. Hours passed as pastries cooled and custard thickened and cooled enough to be placed into the giant pastries. I dusted some of the giant pastries with powdered sugar and drizzled chocolate over them all. After stuffing the refrigerator in the kitchen full of them, I made room for them in the refrigerator outside by the swimming pool. Dawn had arrived bringing its pink and gold clouds before I was finished cooking and filling the éclairs.

When I went back to bed, I was exhausted. I felt as if I had made dessert for an army. When my husband awakened and turned to sit up on his side of the bed, I raised myself and sat up, pretending I had not lain down just one hour earlier.

When my husband sat down for his coffee, I asked, "Would you like a little chocolate éclair?" (I knew he loved sweet pastries in the morning.) I chopped off a huge piece from the custard loaf. "When did you make this?" He ate so happily I didn't feel the need to answer.

That evening after dinner I offered a whipped cream éclair. He said, "Of course." The next day we repeated the actions of the day before except that I gave him whipped cream for breakfast and custard for dinner. The next morning he awakened before I did and left the bedroom. He came back immediately.

"Maya, Maya, wake up. What the hell have we got? Come here."

I followed him to the kitchen. He opened the refrigerator door. Sliced éclairs were stacked on every shelf. He said, "Come outside." He opened the refrigerator door on the deck. "What the hell do we have? An éclair cottage industry?"

"Would you have a bite before you go to work?" I asked.

"No, no. And I'll never eat another éclair as long as I live. I want to see my plate éclair-free when I come home tonight. I know you are having a hard time at your work and I'm sorry. So give them away or you eat them, but I don't fancy dessert made on a crisis-control watch."

I gave most of the éclairs to friends, to staff, and to the soup kitchen at church. But I kept one gargantuan loaf as proof that cooking helps me to write.

I pulled out the stubborn manuscript, which to date had resisted me successfully, and suddenly the words spilled out of my pen and onto the yellow pad.

A few days after my husband had said he never wanted to see another éclair, I offered him a piece of strawberry shortcake. He smiled widely and enjoyed it immensely. He just did not recognize the old éclair simply smothered with strawberries and fresh whipped cream.

ÉCLAIRS ∽

Makes 16 éclairs

250ml/8fl oz/1 cup water

115g/4oz/½ cup (1 stick) butter or
    margarine

¼ teaspoon salt

115g/4oz/1 cup sifted plain
    (all-purpose) flour

50g/2oz/½ cup icing (confectioners')
    sugar

4 large eggs, beaten individually

Custard Filling and/or Golden
    Whipped Cream (recipes follow)

Chocolate Syrup (recipe follows)

Preheat oven to 200°C/400°F/Gas Mark 6.

In large saucepan, heat water, butter and salt to full rolling boil. Reduce heat to low, and quickly stir in flour and icing sugar, mixing vigorously with wooden spoon until mixture leaves the sides of the pan in a ball.

Remove from heat. Add eggs one at a time, beating after each addition until mixture is very smooth. (An electric mixer at a low speed makes this procedure easier.) Pipe mixture or shape mixture with spatula, into 16 fingers, each 2.5 x 10cm/1 x 4in.

Bake on greased baking sheets for 25 to 30 minutes. Remove at once to cooling racks and let cool away from drafts.

Cut the pastries in half lengthwise, spoon onto the bottoms either Custard Filling or Golden Whipped Cream, and replace the tops. Drizzle Chocolate Syrup over the éclairs.

Red Rice

Red Tripe with White Rice

Homemade Biscuits

Hog Head Cheese

Chicken Livers and Buttered Noodles

Black Iron Pot Roast

Smothered Chicken

Ashford Salad '96

CUSTARD FILLING

Fills 8 éclairs

3 large eggs

50g/2oz/¼ cup caster sugar

Pinch of salt

475ml/16fl oz/2 cups milk

½ teaspoon vanilla extract

Beat eggs, sugar, salt and milk until blended in top part of double boiler. Put over simmering water and cook, stirring, for about 7 minutes or until mixture thickens slightly and coats a metal spoon. Remove from hot water and pour into bowl. Add vanilla extract. Cool and chill 1 hour.

GOLDEN WHIPPED CREAM

Fills 8 éclairs

475ml/16fl oz/2 cups whipping cream

150g/5oz/⅔ cup brown sugar

½ teaspoon vanilla extract

Whip cream until it holds peaks. Gradually add brown sugar and vanilla extract. Chill 1 hour.

CHOCOLATE SYRUP

175g/6oz plain or bitter
  (unsweetened) chocolate, melted,
  or 115g/4oz/1 cup cocoa powder

300g/11oz/1½ cups granulated
  sugar

⅛ teaspoon salt

250ml/8fl oz/1 cup boiling water

½ teaspoon vanilla extract

In small saucepan, mix melted chocolate with sugar and salt over low heat. Add boiling water, and cook for 5 minutes, stirring constantly. Cool, add vanilla extract, and refrigerate.

MASSACHUSETTS, TENNESSEE, AND AN ITALIAN SOUP

A group of teachers of foreign languages met in Nashville, Tennessee. The Opryland Hotel was the site of the conference.

The corridors spiking out from the large meeting hall were filled with conversations in Spanish, French, Italian, Japanese, Russian, and some languages I could not recognize.

I had been the morning lecturer and had spoken on the impossibility of successfully translating poetry, yet the imperative that we continue to attempt its translation. The lecture had been well received.

Afterward my assistant and I headed for a restaurant in the hotel. We found a table and ordered coffee. I am much easier to get along with after a few cups of coffee.

Two couples at the next table recognized me, and we began a light and friendly conversation. They were teachers from Springfield, Massachusetts, but had not been a part of the morning's conference. The couples explained that they were best of friends in Massachusetts and that they loved the Opryland Hotel and came on vacation together once a year.

One of the women waved her hands around in the air. "Have you ever seen anything like this?"

I admitted that I had not. It was kitsch at its best and had enough elegance to ward off derision. It was one of the largest hotels in the world. Huge fountains of water arched and fell, dancing to music of Bizet and Haydn. Flowers waved everywhere and restaurants rotated slowly while multicolored birds sang.

Doris, at the next table, said, "But don't order the minestrone. Never order the minestrone."

She said the four of them were Italian Americans and her husband had a rule. If he had had a little too much wine the night before, he liked a hot bowl of minestrone the next day to set him straight. She said he had just ordered it.

"Look at what they served him."

She tilted a soup bowl for me to see. The contents of his bowl looked like cooked oatmeal.

Doris said, "Looks like oatmeal, doesn't it?"

I said, "Yes."

She said, "We'll be back next year, but we just won't order their minestrone."

As soon as she said good-bye, a very trim and handsome young black man came to my table. "Dr. Angelou, we are so honored to have you here in this dining room. Let me introduce myself. I am the manager. Can we do anything for you?"

I said, "No, thank you."

He said, "I want to bring Mr. Williams, he is my manager and manager of the other restaurants here. He'll be so glad to welcome you."

I had finished breakfast, but courtesy kept me in my seat.

The young man returned with an older, elegant black man. He was introduced.

The man said, "We are honored and would love to have you visit some of the larger restaurants, but would you please come to this kitchen and let the workers see you. They will be thrilled."

I followed him into the kitchen, met and shook hands with everyone. My host said, "Now, this is the steam table. Here we keep food hot that has already been cooked."

I looked into the pots. One was filled with something like

oatmeal. The contents were so thick, the ladle stood straight in its middle.

I asked, "And what is this?"

He said, "Oh, that's Minnesota wild rice. It's very popular at lunchtime, but they even had a call for it this morning at breakfast."

Indeed. That was what the woman at the next table had showed me. My impulse was to tell him that my friends from Springfield, Massachusetts, had not meant to order Minnesota wild rice and that maybe what he needed was a good recipe for minestrone for those who might want it on a given morning. I could have suggested that his Tennessee waiters' ears had misunderstood accents from New England and that New England ears did not completely understand Tennessee drawl, but Mr. Williams's smile was so nice and his attitude so welcoming, I didn't have the heart.

MINESTRONE SOUP ∽

Makes about 2 litres/3½ pints/8 cups (2 quarts)

175g/6oz/1 cup dried butter (lima)
   beans
2 litres/3½ pints/8 cups (2 quarts)
   water
50ml/2fl oz/¼ cup olive oil
3 sticks celery, diced
1 medium onion, minced
500g/1¼lb canned crushed tomatoes
225g/8oz/2 cups shredded cabbage
2 garlic cloves, minced
1 teaspoon salt
¼ teaspoon freshly ground black
   pepper
1 teaspoon chopped fresh parsley
½ teaspoon dried basil
½ teaspoon dried oregano
50g/2oz/½ cup dried (elbow) macaroni
   (dried weight), cooked until al
   dente
Grated fresh Parmesan cheese

Pick over beans, discarding stones and debris. Wash and drain, then put in large saucepan with water to cover, bring to boil, and boil for 2 minutes. Let cool for 2 hours.

Heat oil in large skillet, and lightly sauté celery, onion, tomatoes, cabbage and garlic. Add to beans along with salt, pepper and herbs. Cook covered, over medium heat, for 2 to 3 hours.

Before serving, add cooked macaroni to soup. Bring to a boil, and boil for 4 minutes. Serve garnished with Parmesan.

MINNESOTA WILD RICE ∽

Serves 4 to 6

200g/7oz/1 cup uncooked wild rice

475ml/16fl oz/2 cups chicken stock

½ teaspoon salt

1 teaspoon minced onion

50g/2oz/¼ cup (½ stick) butter

¼ teaspoon freshly ground black
    pepper

Wash rice, drain, and cover with water. Bring to a boil, then reduce heat to low immediately. After 20 minutes, add 250ml/8fl oz/1 cup of water, and cook for another 20 minutes. Then rinse and drain again. Pour in chicken stock. Add salt, onion, butter and pepper. Simmer covered until tender and all liquid has evaporated, about 45 minutes.

BLACK IRON POT ROAST

Lee Goldsmith owned a chic cookery store on New York's Upper West Side. She was a striking woman with a sharp wit who knew a lot about cooking. I often found myself in her store either buying a cooking tool or just talking about food and its preparation.

I passed her shop one morning, and through the window I saw her perched on a stool, bent over, her head in her hands and her shoulders heaving. Obviously she was crying. I opened the door.

"What's the matter?"

She did not lift her head.

"Lee, what's the matter?"

She sat up and I saw tears on her face. I also recognized that she wasn't crying. She was caught up in paroxysms of laughter.

I had to wait until she could find and hold a full breath of air. Finally, after many false starts, she said, "A customer came in here, cursed me out, and said she was going to sue me."

Here, laughter took over her again so completely that her body shook.

The story came out in pieces between laughing interruptions.

The woman had come two days earlier and asked if Lee had a heavy black pot for sale. She showed her the item.

The woman asked, "Could you cook a pot roast in this? I have a recipe that I had to steal to get." When Lee answered in the affirmative, the customer asked, "How do you use the pot? Do I have to wash it first?"

Lee explained that any pots or pans sent from a factory must be scrubbed thoroughly to remove a film, which is put on to prevent rust.

The customer asked, "I should wash it?"

Lee said, "Get a Brasso scourer, use a little Ajax, and scrub the pot inside and out. Wash the pot again, and then use Brillo soap pads to scrub it again. When it feels smooth, wash it with regular dish-washing liquid. Dry it with a soft towel. Put some vegetable oil on your hands. Rub that all over the pot and the lid. Put the two into a very slow oven, about 150°F, overnight. Next morning, take it out, let it cool, wash it again lightly, and then continue with your pot roast recipe."

I told Lee that sounded about right. She said yes, except that the customer came into the shop screaming, "You have ruined my life. I followed your instructions and my fiancé brought his parents for dinner last night. His mother makes a killer pot roast and I paid somebody to get her recipe for me. I followed hers as I followed yours, but when I served it they all began to frown and then giggle, and finally they all started laughing. Some of them said they had to pick steel wool out of their teeth."

Lee asked the woman how she had prepared the pot roast.

The customer said, "I did what you suggested. I took the meat and scrubbed with a brass scourer and Ajax. Then I washed it and dried it and washed it again with a soapy Brillo pad. I washed it finally with dish-washing liquid and patted it dry. I put the oil on my hands and rubbed it and put it in a low oven, 150°F, overnight. Yesterday morning I took it out of the oven, and when it was cooled I washed it again and then followed my pot roast recipe.

"I served it last night and they laughed so hard, I put them out of my house – my fiancé and his parents and some friends they had brought with them.

"I'm on my way to send my ring back to the jerk. I never want to hear his name again."

Lee said, "Wait at least a day. No, better wait a week. Do you love him?"

The customer started crying. "Yes."

"Then wait a week. If you can bear to see him, bring him here and I will explain how we miscommunicated." The customer dried her eyes and was a little mollified and said, "I'll think about it. But if I can't forgive him, believe me, I won't forgive you. I will sue your ass."

When Lee and I stopped laughing, she invited me over to her house for pot roast. Hers was delicious.

BLACK IRON POT ROAST ∽

Serves 10 to 12

2.25–2.75kg/5–6lb rolled boneless
    beef chuck, chuck blade or
    shoulder
Salt and freshly ground black pepper,
    to taste
3 tablespoons plain (all-purpose) flour
1 tablespoon vegetable oil
1 large onion, studded with 5 cloves
3 carrots, peeled and cut into large
    pieces
1 stick celery, cut into large pieces
250ml/8fl oz/1 cup water or beef
    stock
3 tablespoons cornflour (cornstarch)
    mixed with 3 tablespoons water

Preheat oven to 180°C/350°F/Gas Mark 4.

Season meat with salt and pepper; then dust lightly with flour.

In large flameproof casserole dish with tight-fitting lid, brown meat slowly on all sides in hot oil. Add onion, carrots, celery and water.

Cover tightly, and bake for 2 hours, or until meat is very tender. Check casserole every half hour, adding water if needed. Do not allow meat to burn.

Remove meat. Thicken liquid with a cornflour-and-water paste for gravy. Serve with boiled and buttered potatoes.

OPRAH'S SUFFOCATED CHICKEN

I gave a series of seminars at a university in Maryland. On my last day, a fifth request for an interview was about to receive the same negative response I had given the other four.

"I appreciate the request, but I have a plane to catch ..."

The voice said, "Doctor, I only need five minutes of your time. You have my word you will be free to go in five minutes." She sounded so cool and definite.

I asked, "Do you want me to come to your studio?"

"No, Dr. Angelou, I will bring my crew to you and I won't disturb you until we are set up and I am ready to shoot. I give you my word."

I was won over. Anybody can find five minutes in a day despite its other demands. The reporter told me her name, but it didn't catch in my memory. I said yes and gave her a time.

When I informed my host at the university that I had agreed to give an interview, he asked why after having refused the other requests. I answered, "I rarely find young people today (and she sounds young) who know that one's word is a powerful thing and that it can be given or it can be withheld." That television journalist had impressed me enough to make me curious to see how good her word was.

The next day when I concluded my seminar, an attractive young woman opened the classroom door.

"Dr. Angelou?"

"Yes."

"I am here to do the interview. My crew is set up. We are ready if you are!"

I followed her to the next room and she pointed out a chair. She had put a pillow in the chair so that the camera could be level to my face. I sat. She looked at her watch and automatically I looked at mine. She nodded and the crew leapt to attention. She asked one question, and I was so surprised at its complexity and relevance that it engaged my total attention. She really listened to my answer and her second question stemmed from my response.

She looked at her watch and said, "Thank you, Dr. Angelou."

My watch told me that exactly five minutes had passed.

I told her that because of our hurried telephone conversation the day before I had not really caught her name.

She said, "Oprah Winfrey."

I said, "Young woman, you will go far. I hope to be around to see your success."

A few years later I attended a social affair in Chicago and I saw her standing on the side. I walked over and said, "Hello, Oprah Winfrey. How are you?"

She said, "You remember me, and you remembered my name."

I said, "Of course. You are going to do wonderful things in your lifetime."

She had been offered her own show in Chicago and had accepted. She knew that Phil Donahue was the most popular daytime host in the nation and that he also broadcasted from Chicago. Donahue would be formidable competition.

I gave her my card and invited her to come and visit me in North Carolina.

One month later, she came and brought her gentleman friend. I served smothered chicken and rice, which was well received.

After dinner the first night we sat on the floor and read poetry. Her delight in the beauty of the spoken word pleased me. I told her that all poetry was music written for the human voice. We recited long into the night.

The next morning as I was planning breakfast for my houseguests, she came pajamaed into the kitchen.

She said, "Your house feels like home."

I said, "I hope you will always think that."

I told her that the poet Robert Frost had said, "Home is where when you go there, no one can put you out."

I said, "I offer you this home whenever you need it or even if you just want it.

"Would you like eggs and bacon? Grits and sausage? Ham and green tomatoes?"

She laughed and said she'd like some of the previous night's dinner of chicken and biscuits.

At the table she asked, "What do you call this dish?" She pointed to the chicken.

I said, "That's smothered chicken."

She said, "No, this is too good for such a simple name. This is suffocated chicken." She then added, "This chicken never knew what hit it."

SMOTHERED CHICKEN

Serves 8

Two 1.3kg/3lb (fryer) chickens

Juice of 2 lemons

½ teaspoon salt

½ teaspoon freshly ground black
    pepper

115g/4oz/1 cup plain (all-purpose)
    flour

115g/4oz/½ cup (1 stick) butter

120ml/4fl oz/½ cup vegetable oil

2 medium onions, sliced

450g/1lb button mushrooms, sliced

1 clove garlic, minced

475ml/16fl oz/2 cups chicken broth or
    chicken stock

Wash and pat dry chickens. Cut into pieces, and put in a bowl with lemon juice and water to cover. Refrigerate for 1 hour.

Wash lemon water off chicken, and season with salt and pepper. Dredge pieces in 90g/3½oz/¾ cup flour.

In large skillet, fry chicken pieces on high heat in butter and 50ml/2fl oz/¼ cup oil until dark brown. Remove from skillet.

Add remaining flour and oil to skillet. Cook flour until brown. Add onions, mushrooms and garlic, stirring constantly. Put chicken back into skillet. Add chicken broth and water to cover. Turn heat to medium, and cook for 25 minutes.

Serve with Buttermilk Biscuits (p. 40).

ASHFORD SALAD '96

A dinner without meat can satisfy. Prepared with skill, it can even delight. But I did not know that when I was a child. I grew up during an impoverished time and in a poor part of the United States.

The Depression, which assailed the entire country, hit the South with a particularly heavy blow. Poor people who lived in a cotton economy and who were happy to have fresh meat once a month were challenged to find enough work to put the sparest vegetarian dinners on their tables.

Those who were used to eating fresh meat at least twice a week were challenged to find the resources to buy it twice a month.

I belonged to the first group, and although we did have chickens and cured meat, vegetables dominated our meals, whether we wished it or not. Inventive cooks found ways to use the cured meat that was included in their cooked dishes. Each pot of greens was stewed with as much smoked or cured meat as the cook could afford. Country ham slices and boiled bacon slabs were offered at least once a week, and one could be assured that it was definitely chicken on Sunday.

After I grew up and away from the days of poverty and the southern place of need, I found that I often wished for a meatless dinner of crunchy vegetables and an oven-roasted Irish potato, or pasta with a fresh tomato sauce. However, until I met Valerie Simpson and Nick Ashford I had never thought it could be exciting to be creative in cooking vegetarian food. The songwriting couple came to visit me in North Carolina, and within hours they had taken my heart. I could think of nothing more pleasing than to please them. Valerie would eat chicken and fish, but Nick was a definite vegetarian. I bought the prepared dishes made of soybeans from the supermarket. They were concocted of mushrooms and oats and rice. I tasted them and they were horrible. I decided I would simply try to cook vegetables so well that the diner would prefer my dish to a standing rib roast. I know that was wishful thinking but I also knew that good veggies well prepared could please any palate.

First I offered a dish called chakchouka in North Africa and ratatouille in France. Then I served a tomato soufflé with snow peas and celery gratin as side dishes. Nick loved it. One day I offered a salad that Nick liked so much I named it the Ashford '96.

When I served another mixed salad with feta and golden raisins, not only did Nick decide that I was one of the best cooks he had ever known, he had to know the exact measurements in all my salad recipes.

The Ashford-Simpsons were a bright and beautiful couple, quick and funny, and I had long admired their talent, but their shared laughter, love, and gentle personalities won them to my heart. I gave the recipes to them a number of times, but they swore they could not replicate the dishes.

When they visit me in North Carolina and when I go see them in New York, they look at me with such large, longing eyes that without being asked I will go to the kitchen and make one of "Nick's green salads."

Here are the recipes for the salads and other vegetarian dishes I created for Nick Ashford.

TOMATO SOUFFLÉ ∽

Serves 8

Six 400g/14oz cans crushed
    tomatoes
65g/2½oz/5 tablespoons butter
½ teaspoon granulated sugar
½ teaspoon salt, plus a pinch of salt
4 slices white bread, torn into
    medium-size pieces
2 tablespoons plain (all-purpose) flour
1 teaspoon cornflour (cornstarch)
250ml/8fl oz/1 cup cold milk
5 large eggs, separated

Sauté tomatoes in large skillet with 25g/1oz/2 tablespoons butter, the sugar and ¼ teaspoon salt until dry. Add bread, and mix well. Cool.

Preheat oven to 180°C/350°F/Gas Mark 4.

Use 15g/½oz/1 tablespoon butter to grease soufflé dish. Sprinkle ¼ teaspoon salt in soufflé dish so that it coats bottom and sides.

Melt remaining butter in large saucepan over medium heat. Add flour and cornflour, and stir for 1 minute. Add milk all at once. Stir. Remove from heat. Add egg yolks into mixture one at a time. Add sautéed tomatoes, mixing well.

In a clean, dry bowl, whisk whites of eggs with pinch of salt until stiff. Fold into soufflé mixture carefully. Pour mixture into soufflé dish, filling it three-quarters full. Bake for 35 minutes, or until puffed and golden. Serve immediately.

CHAKCHOUKA (MOROCCAN STEW)

Serves 8 to 10

6 tablespoons olive oil

2 large aubergines (eggplant), peeled and cut into 5cm/2in pieces

1 large onion, sliced

2 green (bell) peppers, seeded and cut into large pieces

1 red (bell) pepper, seeded and cut into large pieces

2 courgettes (zucchini), cut into large pieces

2 yellow squash or 2 yellow courgettes (zucchini), cut into large pieces

4 tomatoes, skinned and chopped

4 cloves garlic, minced

Salt and freshly ground black pepper, to taste

Heat oil in large, heavy-based saucepan. Add aubergines, and fry for 4 to 5 minutes. Add onion, and sauté until translucent. Add remaining ingredients and stir, then cover and cook over medium-low heat for 25 minutes, stirring frequently. Check seasonings and adjust if needed.

ASHFORD SALAD '96 ∽

Serves 6 to 8

2 heads romaine lettuce, with tough
    outer leaves removed

4 tablespoons extra-virgin olive oil

3 tablespoons fresh lemon juice

2 tablespoons red wine vinegar

1 tablespoon caster sugar

2 cloves garlic, finely minced

Salt and freshly ground black pepper,
    to taste

1 ripe avocado, peeled, stoned and
    diced

1 large ripe tomato, cut into small
    wedges

1 large (English) cucumber, sliced

Wash lettuce, dry, wrap in paper towels, and put into refrigerator. Mix oil, lemon juice, vinegar, sugar and garlic in large salad bowl. Season with salt and pepper. Mash avocado with potato masher, and mix with ingredients in salad bowl. Check seasonings. Mix in tomato and cucumber. Just before serving, remove lettuce from refrigerator. Break into large pieces, and toss into salad bowl. With salad tongs, mix vigorously until each lettuce leaf has been flavoured with dressing.

MIXED SALAD WITH FETA AND GOLDEN RAISINS ∽

Serves 4

1 head Little Gem (Bibb) lettuce

1 bunch watercress

150g/5oz/1 cup sultanas (golden
    raisins)

2 tablespoons extra-virgin olive oil

3 tablespoons fresh lemon juice

½ tablespoon balsamic vinegar

1 teaspoon finely minced fresh garlic

salt and freshly ground black pepper,
    to taste

115g/4oz/1 cup crumbled feta cheese

Remove and discard old leaves from lettuce and watercress; then wash. Wrap in paper towels and refrigerate. Put sultanas into small pan with water to cover, and simmer for 3 minutes. Take off heat and set aside so sultanas can plump up. In large salad bowl, place oil, lemon juice, vinegar and garlic. Season with salt and pepper. Mix well. Just before serving, remove greens from refrigerator, and tear into large pieces. Drain sultanas, discarding water. Mix dressing and sultanas and greens, and sprinkle feta cheese on top. Serve at once.

INDEX

appetizers
  Hog Head Cheese, 170
  Moulded Eggs Polignac,
    126
  Pâté, 125
  Pickled Pig's Feet, or
    Souse, 169
apples
  Fried Apples, 138
  Roasted Capon, 86
  Smoked Pork Chops, 70
Ashford Salad '96, 211
aubergines, Chakchouka
    (Moroccan Stew), 210
avocados, Ashford Salad
    '96, 211

bacon
  Bailey's Smothered Pork
    Chops, 69
  Liver and Onions, 46
  Red Rice, 86
  Wilted Lettuce, 51
Bailey's Smothered Pork
    Chops, 69
Banana Pudding, 92
beans, dried
  Bob's Boston Baked
    Beans, 146
  Cassoulet, 152
  Minestrone Soup, 190
beans, fresh, Haricots
    Verts, 164
beef
  Beef Wellington, 160
  Black Iron Pot Roast,
    198
  Braised Short Ribs of
    Beef, 81

Momma's Rich Beef
    Stew, 28
Braised Cabbage with
    Ginger, 71
Braised Short Ribs of
    Beef, 79
Cabbage with Celery
    and Water Chestnuts,
    72
Chakchouka (Moroccan
    Stew), 210
Chicken and Dumplings,
    8
Gazpacho, 161
Hog Head Cheese, 170
Momma's Rich Beef
    Stew, 28
Pickled Pig's Feet, or
    Souse, 169
Red Rice, 86
biscuits
  Buttermilk Biscuits, 40
  Fried Meat Pies, 58
  Homemade Biscuits, 139
Black Iron Pot Roast, 198
Bob's Boston Baked
    Beans, 146
Bouquet Garni, 9
Braised Cabbage with
    Ginger, 71
Braised Short Ribs of Beef,
    79
Bread Pudding, 64
breads
  Buttermilk Biscuits, 40
  Crackling Corn Bread,
    27
  Homemade Biscuits, 139
  Spoon Bread, 138

butter
  Buttered Noodles, 176
  Pâté, 125
  Buttermilk Biscuits, 40

cabbage
  Braised Cabbage with
    Ginger, 71
  Cabbage with Celery
    and Water Chestnuts,
    72
  Minestrone Soup, 190
cakes
  Caramel Cake, 19
  Coconut Cake, 21
candy, Chocolate Fudge,
    22
capon, Roasted Capon, 86
Caramel Cake, 19
Caramel Icing, 20
Caramel Syrup, 20
carrots
  Braised Short Ribs of
    Beef, 79
  Momma's Rich Beef
    Stew, 28
  Tripe à la Mode de Caen,
    99
Cassoulet, 152
celery
  Bouquet Garni, 9
  Braised Short Ribs of
    Beef, 79
  Cabbage with Celery
    and Water Chestnuts,
    72
  Cassoulet, 152
  Cold Potato Salad, 36
  Corn Bread Stuffing, 117

Hog Head Cheese, 170
Chakchouka (Moroccan
    Stew), 210
cheddar cheese, Twice-
    Baked Potatoes, 163
cheese. See cheddar cheese;
    feta cheese
chicken
  Cassoulet, 152
  Chicken and Dumplings,
    8
  Decca's Chicken,
    Drunkard Style, 145
  Fried Chicken, 37
  Fried Meat Pies, 58
  Roasted Capon, 86
  Smothered Chicken, 204
  Tamales de Maiz con
    Pollo (Green
    Cornhusk Tamales
    with Chicken Filling),
    108
chicken liver
  Chicken Livers, 175
  Pâté, 125
chillies
  Collard Greens, 29
  Menudos (Tripe Stew), 101
chocolate
  Chocolate Fudge, 21
  Chocolate Syrup, 183
cilantro, Tamales de Maiz
    con Pollo (Green
    Cornhusk Tamales
    with Chicken Filling),
    108
coconut
  Coconut Cake, 21
  Coconut Icing, 22

cognac, Pâté, 125
Cold Potato Salad, 36
Collard Greens, 29
Corn Bread Stuffing, 117
cornhusks, Tamales de
    Maiz con Pollo (Green
    Cornhusk Tamales
    with Chicken Filling),
    108
cornmeal
    Corn Bread Stuffing, 117
    Crackling Corn Bread,
    27
    Spoon Bread, 138
Crackling Corn Bread, 27
cream
    Green Peas and Lettuce,
    10
    Onion Tart, 132
cucumbers
    Ashford Salad '96, 211
    Gazpacho, 161
Custard Filling, 183

Decca's Chicken,
    Drunkard Style, 145
Drop Dumplings, 9
duck, Cassoulet, 152
duck livers, Pâté, 125
dumplings
    Chicken and Dumplings,
    8
    Drop Dumplings, 9

Éclairs, 182
eggs
    Banana Pudding, 92
    Bread Pudding, 64
    Cold Potato Salad, 36
    Lemon Meringue Pie, 7
    Meringue, 7
    Moulded Eggs Polignac,
    126
    Onion Tart, 132
    Spoon Bread, 138
    Tomato Soufflé, 209

feta cheese, Mixed Salad
    with Feta and Golden
    Raisins, 211
Filling, Custard, 183
Fried Apples, 138
Fried Chicken, 37
Fried Meat Pies, 58
Fried Yellow Summer
    Squash, 9

Fudge, Chocolate, 22
Gazpacho, 161
ginger, Braised Cabbage
    with Ginger, 71
Golden Whipped Cream,
    183
goose, Cassoulet, 152
goose livers, Pâté, 125
Great Northern beans,
    Bob's Boston Baked
    Beans, 146
green beans. See beans,
    fresh
Green Peas and Lettuce,
    10
green peppers
greens
    Braised Cabbage with
    Ginger, 71
    Cabbage with Celery
    and Water Chestnuts,
    72
    Collard Greens, 29
    Mustard and Turnip
    Greens with Smoked
    Turkey Wings, 38
    Wilted Lettuce, 51
    See also lettuce

Haricots Verts, 164
Hog Head Cheese, 170
Homemade Biscuits, 139
hominy, Menudos (Tripe
    Stew), 101
hot peppers. See chillies

icings
    Caramel icing, 20
    Coconut icing, 22

lamb, Cassoulet, 152
lemons
    Fried Chicken, 37
    Lemon Meringue Pie, 7
    Menudos (Tripe Stew),
    101
lettuce
    Ashford Salad '96, 211
    Green Peas and Lettuce,
    10
    Mixed Salad with Feta
    and Golden Raisins,
    211
    Wilted Lettuce, 51
lima beans, Minestrone
    Soup, 190

liver
    Chicken Livers, 175
    Liver and Onions, 46
    Pâté, 125
macaroni, Minestrone
    Soup, 190
masa, Tamales de Maiz con
    Pollo (Green
    Cornhusk Tamales
    with Chicken Filling),
    108
mayonnaise, Cold Potato
    Salad, 36
Menudos (Tripe Stew), 101
Meringue, 7
milk
    Bread Pudding, 64
    Petit Pois, 162
    Tomato Soufflé, 209
Minestrone Soup, 190
Minnesota Wild Rice, 191
Mixed Salad with Feta and
    Golden Raisins, 211
molasses, Bob's Boston
    Baked Beans, 146
Moulded Eggs Polignac,
    126
Momma's Rich Beef Stew,
    28
mushrooms
    Beef Wellington, 160
    Smothered Chicken, 204
    Veal Medallions, 124
Mustard and Turnip
    Greens with Smoked
    Turkey Wings, 38

Noodles, Buttered, 176
onions
    Bailey's Smothered Pork
    Chops, 69
    Beef Wellington, 160
    Bob's Boston Baked
    Beans, 146
    Braised Short Ribs of
    Beef, 79
    Cassoulet, 152
    Chakchouka (Moroccan
    Stew), 210
    Cold Potato Salad, 36
    Decca's Chicken,
    Drunkard Style, 145
    Fried Meat Pies, 58
    Fried Yellow Summer
    Squash, 9
    Gazpacho, 161

Liver and Onions, 46
Menudos (Tripe Stew), 101
Minestrone Soup, 190
Onion Tart, 132
Pâté, 125
Petit Pois, 162
Pickled Pig's Feet, or
    Souse, 169
Red Tripe with White
    Rice, 100
Smothered Chicken,
    204
Tamales de Maiz con
    Pollo (Green
    Cornhusk Tamales
    with Chicken Filling),
    108
Tripe à la Mode de Caen,
    99
orange juice, Pickled
    Peaches, 39

parsley, Veal Medallions,
    124
parsnips, Momma's Rich
    Beef Stew, 28
pastry
    Éclairs, 182
    Puffed Pastry, 161
Pâté, 125
    Beef Wellington, 160
pea beans, Cassoulet, 152
peaches, Pickled Peaches,
    39
peas
    Green Peas and Lettuce,
    10
    Petit Pois, 162
peppers. See green
    peppers; chillies
Petit Pois, 162
Pickled Peaches, 39
Pickled Pig's Feet, or
    Souse, 169
pies and tarts
    Fried Meat Pies, 58
    Lemon Meringue Pie, 7
    Onion Tart, 132
pig's ears, Hog Head
    Cheese, 170
pig's feet
    Hog Head Cheese, 170
    Pickled Pig's Feet, or
    Souse, 169
pineapple, Smoked Pork
    Chops, 70

pork
  Bailey's Smothered Pork
    Chops, 69
  Cassoulet, 152
  Fried Meat Pies, 58
  Hog Head Cheese, 170
  Pickled Pig's Feet, or
    Souse, 169
  Sausage, 140
  Smoked Pork Chops,
    70
potatoes
  Cold Potato Salad, 36
  Momma's Rich Beef
    Stew, 28
  Twice-Baked Potatoes,
    163
Pot Roast, Black Iron, 198
pudding
  Banana Pudding, 92
  Bread Pudding, 64
Puffed Pastry, 161

raisins
  Bread Pudding, 64
  Mixed Salad with Feta
    and Golden Raisins,
    211
Red Rice, 86
Red Tripe with White
  Rice, 100
rice
  Minnesota Wild Rice,
    191
  Red Rice, 86
  Red Tripe with White
    Rice, 100
Roasted Capon, 86
Roasted Turkey, 116

sage, Corn Bread Stuffing,
  117

salad dressings
  Vinaigrette, 164
salads
  Ashford Salad '96, 211
  Cold Potato Salad, 36
  Mixed Salad with Feta
    and Golden Raisins,
    211
  Wilted Lettuce, 51
salt pork
  Bob's Boston Baked
    Beans, 146
  Cassoulet, 152
  Tripe à la Mode de Caen,
    99
sausage
  Cassoulet, 152
  Sausage, 140
sherry, Chicken Livers,
  175
short ribs, Braised Short
  Ribs of Beef, 79
Smoked Pork Chops, 70
Smothered Chicken, 204
Snow-White Turnips, 38
Soufflé, Tomato, 209
soups
  Gazpacho, 161
  Minestrone Soup, 190
soured cream, Twice-
  Baked Potatoes, 163
Souse, Pickled Pig's Feet,
  169
Spoon Bread, 138
stews
  Chakchouka (Moroccan
    Stew), 210
  Chicken and Dumplings,
    8
  Menudos (Tripe Stew), 101
  Momma's Rich Beef
    Stew, 28

Smothered Chicken, 204
Stuffing, Corn Bread, 117
summer squash
  Chakchouka (Moroccan
    Stew), 210
  Fried Yellow Summer
    Squash, 9
Swedes, Momma's Rich
  Beef Stew, 28
sweet relish, Cold Potato
  Salad, 36
syrups
  Caramel Syrup, 20
  Chocolate Syrup, 183

Tamales de Maiz con Pollo
  (Green Cornhusk
  Tamales with Chicken
  Filling), 108
Tart, Onion, 132
tomatoes
  Ashford Salad '96, 211
  Braised Short Ribs of
    Beef, 79
  Cassoulet, 152
  Chakchouka (Moroccan
    Stew), 210
  Gazpacho, 161
  Minestrone Soup, 190
  Red Rice, 86
  Red Tripe with White
    Rice, 100
  Tomato Soufflé, 209
tripe
  Menudos (Tripe Stew),
    101
  Red Tripe with White
    Rice, 100
  Tripe à la Mode de Caen,
    99
truffles, Moulded Eggs
  Polignac, 126

turkey
  Collard Greens, 29
  Mustard and Turnip
    Greens with Smoked
    Turkey Wings, 38
  Roasted Turkey, 116
turnip greens, Mustard and
  Turnip Greens with
  Smoked Turkey
  Wings, 38
turnips
  Momma's Rich Beef
    Stew, 28
  Snow-White Turnips, 38
Twice-Baked Potatoes, 163

vanilla wafer cookies
  Banana Pudding, 92
veal
  Pâté, 125
  Veal Medallions, 124
Vinaigrette, 164

water chestnuts, Cabbage
  with Celery and Water
  Chestnuts, 72
whipping cream
  Coconut Icing, 22
  Golden Whipped
    Cream, 183
Wilted Lettuce, 51
wine
  Braised Short Ribs of
    Beef, 79
  Cassoulet, 152
  Decca's Chicken,
    Drunkard Style, 145
  Hog Head Cheese, 170
  Tripe à la Mode de Caen,
    99
  Veal Medallions, 124